KIDS COOKING MADE Easy

Richmond Cheder Prize Giving 2017

Awarded to
Leah Katz

For
working hard and always coming to lessons with enthusiasm

Donated by Geoffrey Baum in loving memory of his Brother
Prof. David Baum

LEAH SCHAPIRA & VICTORIA DWEK

FOOD STYLIST AMIT FARBER
PHOTOGRAPHY DANIEL LAILAH

DESIGN RACHELADLERDESIGN.COM
PUBLISHER MESORAH PUBLICATIONS, LTD.

© Copyright 2013 by **Mesorah Publications, Ltd.**

First Edition — First Impression / October 2013

ALL RIGHTS RESERVED

No part of this book may be reproduced in any form, photocopy, electronic media, or otherwise — even for personal, study group, or classroom use — without written permission from the copyright holder, except by a reviewer who wishes to quote brief passages in connection with a review written for inclusion in magazines or newspapers.

THE RIGHTS OF THE COPYRIGHT HOLDER WILL BE STRICTLY ENFORCED.

Published by **ARTSCROLL / SHAAR PRESS**
4401 Second Avenue / Brooklyn, NY 11232 / (718) 921-9000
www.artscroll.com

Distributed in Israel by **SIFRIATI / A. GITLER**
6 Hayarkon Street / Bnei Brak 51127 / Israel

Distributed in Europe by **LEHMANNS**
Unit E, Viking Business Park, Rolling Mill Road
Jarrow, Tyne and Wear, NE32 3DP / England

Distributed in Australia and New Zealand by **GOLDS WORLD OF JUDAICA**
3-13 William Street / Balaclava, Melbourne 3183, Victoria / Australia

Distributed in South Africa by **KOLLEL BOOKSHOP**
Ivy Common / 105 William Road / Norwood 2192 / Johannesburg, South Africa

ISBN-10: 1-4226-1435-2 / ISBN-13: 978-1-4226-1435-8

Printed in the Canada by NOBLE BOOK PRESS

ACKNOWLEDGMENTS

WE ALWAYS SAY THAT OUR IDEAS AREN'T OURS.

We can be totally stumped, but then **Hashem** inserts something brilliant into our heads. We owe Him credit for every little teaspoon in this book.

To the **Schapira** and **Dwek** kids—**C**, **F**, **PY**, **L**, and even little **CA** ... and **Y**, **Y**, **Y**, and little princess **R**. You're our most important taste-testers. It's all about making you happy!

We hope you had fun tasting and testing. We're almost ready to let you take over the cooking.

Thanks also to our husbands, our encouraging parents, and the rest of our families.

To the neighborhood kids, who helped us brainstorm, especially the **Siegfrieds**, **Lubins**, **Wiesenfelds**, and **Krigers**.

Thanks to our brilliant creative team: our stylist, **Amit Farber**; our photographer, **Daniel Lailah**; our designer **Rachel Adler**; and our operations manager, **Zalman Roth**.

Thanks to the **ArtScroll** team: **Gedaliah Zlotowitz**, editor **Felice Eisner**, designers **Eli Kroen** and **Devorah Bloch**, proofreaders **Judi Dick** and **Tova Ovits**, and to the rest of the staff who kept things moving.

Thanks to the cookkosher members who keep on stimulating us with their ideas.

Whenever we were inspired by a cookkosher member's contribution, you'll find the member's name on the recipe page. In appreciation, they'll each be receiving a copy of this cookbook.

We hope you enjoy these delicious, tried and true recipes, and that they motivate you to have fun creating delicious meals for your families. And we hope we've made it easy, too.

ON THE COVER:
In the roll: **CHICKEN WITH DIY BARBECUE SAUCE**, *page 40.*

On the right: **ONION N' GARLIC POPCORN**, *page 80.*

On the left: **SKINNY BERRY COOLATA**, *page 92.*

INTRODUCTION

VICTORIA: How did we decide what kinds of food should be in a cookbook for kids?

LEAH: We sat outside my house with a pen and a pad of paper.

VICTORIA: And a big megaphone. We announced, "Come here and tell us what you like to eat!"

LEAH: There was really no megaphone. Word travels fast. Once the kids in the neighborhood heard we were taking suggestions for our next book, they all came running. Soon, kids 8 and up lined up to tell us what they love to eat, what they like to buy (although their mothers don't always let them), and what they wish they could make themselves.

VICTORIA: The boys wanted meat. Like Sino Steak Sandwiches (page 46). And the girls wanted Skinny Berry Coolatas (page 92).

LEAH: And we made sure to include all their favorites. But you don't need to be a kid to love this book.

VICTORIA: You can be a hungry adult.

LEAH: Or you can be a new cook, a teen, a parent who needs to cook for kids ... or a kid-at-heart.

VICTORIA: If you do happen to be a kid, and you think that you can't cook, you will learn very quickly that you can.

LEAH: I started cooking at age 8. Before then, I pretty much ate pizza for breakfast, lunch, and supper. The classic picky eater. My mother didn't think that was too healthy. Out of desperation, she thought that maybe if I helped her cook, I might discover new foods I liked.

VICTORIA: Did it work?

LEAH: Slowly. I learned that if I like French fries, which are made of potatoes, then why not try roasted potatoes too?

VICTORIA: I wasn't allowed in the kitchen. My mom was worried I'd make a mess.

LEAH: C'mon, Victoria. You didn't even cook once?

VICTORIA: Once. One time, when I was a kid, I made a spaghetti pie. Huge mess.

LEAH: Warning to kids: Clean up after yourself and your mother will let you cook again.

VICTORIA: When I finally did try to start cooking, I didn't know how to scramble eggs or boil pasta. Once I mastered those, I learned everything else simply by following recipes. And you will too. Every time you try a recipe in this book, you'll pick up new cooking tips.

LEAH: While creating this book, we tried to please two types of kids: the picky pizza-loving kid (me). And the sophisticated teen (that's you, Victoria).

VICTORIA: Yes, I was that salad and fat-free muffin-loving teen.

LEAH: So we really understand you all.

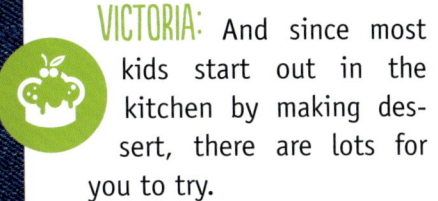

VICTORIA: And since most kids start out in the kitchen by making dessert, there are lots for you to try.

LEAH: You might never be bored again. Next time it's raining, keep busy with our "Sweets and Crafts" chapter.

VICTORIA: To parents of picky eaters: This book could be your solution. If your kids are too young to help, let them look at the photos and pick their favorites. (The adults in the house won't mind a turn to choose their favorites too.)

LEAH: Once those kids are old enough, you can also bring them into the kitchen like my mother did. Kids feel so confident and so proud when they learn to prepare their first dishes on their own.

VICTORIA: And if you're not the type of parent that likes building Lego towers, cooking is a way to spend productive time together.

LEAH: Then kids and adults both will enjoy the best part: The greatest satisfaction in cooking is making other people happy. Nothing beats that.

BEYOND MEASURE

CUP CONVERSIONS

- ¼ cup + ¼ cup = ½ cup
- ⅓ cup + ⅓ cup = ⅔ cup
- ½ cup + ¼ cup = ¾ cup
- ½ cup + ½ cup = 1 cup

OUNCES CONVERSIONS

Sometime, liquids are measured in ounces instead of cups:

- 1 cup = 8 ounces
- 1 pint = 2 cups = 16 ounces
- 1 quart = 2 pints = 32 ounces
- 1 gallon = 4 quarts = 128 ounces

SPOON CONVERSIONS

- 5½ tablespoons = ⅓ cup
- 4 tablespoons = ¼ cup
- 2 tablespoons = ⅛ cup
- 3 teaspoons = 1 tablespoon
- pinch = less than ⅛ teaspoon

WET

Use a measuring cup with a spout for liquids. It's easy to pour from, the liquid won't spill out, and there are measurements on the side of the cup so you can see the quantity you have inside.

DRY

Use this kind of measuring cup for dry ingredients. Fill it up and level off the top.

ABBREVIATIONS

Don't get confused by abbreviations:

1 tablespoon = 1 Tbsp = 1 T
1 teaspoon = 1 tsp = 1 t
1 pound = 1 lb
1 ounce = 1 oz

STICK CONVERSIONS

¼ stick margarine
=
2 tablespoons
=
⅛ cup
=
1 ounce

½ stick margarine
=
4 tablespoons
=
¼ cup
=
2 ounces

1 stick margarine
=
8 tablespoons
=
½ cup
=
4 ounces

ONION

Begin cutting an onion by slicing off the top and bottom, removing the outer papery layer, and slicing your onion in half from stem to root. After that, you can cut your onion many different ways.

SLICED
Cut your onion into thin strips across the long side.

FRENCHED
Cut your onion into thin strips on an angle across the short side.

FINELY DICED
Chop across your onion strips, about ¼ inch apart.

DICED
Chop across your onion strips, about ½ inch apart.

SAUTÉED ONION

SOFT
Onions sautéed about 5-7 minutes

LIGHTLY GOLDEN
Onions sautéed about 12-15 minutes

GARLIC

MINCED
Use a knife or a mini chopper to mince your garlic.

FROZEN GARLIC CUBES
Each cube is equal to about 1 garlic clove.

DEEPLY GOLDEN & CARAMELIZED
Onions sautéed about 20 minutes

CRUSHED
Use a garlic press to crush your garlic.

SLICED
Use a knife to slice your garlic.

FRESH GARLIC CLOVES
Fresh is always best, but garlic can be a pain to peel. Some stores sell fresh garlic cloves pre-peeled for convenience.

SET YOUR TABLE

THE BASIC RULE of thumb for all place settings is to "begin at the outside and work in." Utensils should be placed in the order that they'll be used; the farthest one from the plate is used first; the utensils closest to the plate are used last. On the left, the smaller appetizer fork would be farther from the plate than the dinner fork. On the right, the soup spoon, used in one of the first courses, would be farther away than the knife.

"Knife" and "spoon" go on the "right" = 5 letters
"Fork" goes on the "left" = 4 letters

Drinking glasses go on the top right side of the plate. If you'll be placing a roll at each plate, it can go on the top left side.

Place knives with their cutting edge toward the plate and make sure all of the utensil handles line up at the bottom.

BEFORE AND AFTER COOKING

1. Have all your ingredients "mise en place." That's the French term for having all your ingredients ready before you begin to cook. It means "putting in place." Make sure you have the right quantity of each ingredient. Measure, wash, and chop before you begin.

2. Read the instructions through before you start to cook. You'll see if there are any steps where you need an adult's help, and if you'll have time to complete the recipe. The icons at the top of the page will tell you if you will need sharp knives, a mixer or blender, the oven, or the stovetop.

3. Whenever a recipe calls for "salt," we used kosher salt. If you only have table salt at home, you'll need much less, about ½ teaspoon for every 1 teaspoon kosher salt. Stir thoroughly and taste your food to make sure it is well seasoned.

4. If you want to make only half of a recipe, make sure you halve every ingredient. Cooking temperature will be the same, but the cooking time might be shorter.

WHILE THEY'RE EATING Stay humble and let the food talk. Don't tell others how awesome your dish is. Let them taste and be surprised by how well you can really cook

AFTER YOU COOK Clean up so mom will let you cook again. Better yet, clean up as you go along.

HANDY HALVES

ORGINAL	HALF
1 cup	½ cup
¾ cup	¼ cup + 2 Tbsp
⅔ cup	⅓ cup
½ cup	¼ cup
⅓ cup	2 Tbsp + 2 tsp
¼ cup	2 Tbsp
3 Tbsp	1 Tbsp + 1½ tsp
2 Tbsp	1 Tbsp
1 Tbsp	1½ tsp

KNIFE OVEN STOVETOP MICROWAVE
 MIXER BLENDER/FOOD PROCESSOR GRILL SANDWICH MAKER

Look here to see what advanced kitchen tools or appliances you'll need to make each recipe.

These icons near the recipe correspond to the recipe notes on the right.

PANINI WRAPS

This tells you how many servings or the quantity the recipe will make.

YIELD: 4 SERVINGS

WHILE we were creating recipes for this book, one mom had a request: "My teenage daughters and their friends want to know what they can prepare for lunch. They want healthy ideas that are also delicious." Well, girls, take out your panini maker, because your wraps are about to get a big upgrade. –V.

INGREDIENTS

- 2 red peppers
- 3 Tbsp cream cheese
- 4 whole wheat wraps
- 4 tsp chopped fresh basil (or 4 frozen cubes, thawed)
- 1 avocado, sliced
- 4 oz feta or mozzarella cheese
- 4 cups lettuce

PANINI DIP:
- ¼ cup mayonnaise
- 2 Tbsp vinegar
- 1 Tbsp water
- 1 tsp garlic
- 1 tsp sugar

INSTRUCTIONS

1. Preheat oven to 400°F. Place red peppers into a baking pan and roast until the skin appears blistered (there should be some black marks all around), 35-40 minutes. Remove from oven and let cool. Once cool, the skin should peel off easily. Cut peeled peppers into strips

2. Spread cream cheese across the bottom-center of each wrap. Top with basil, red pepper strips, avocado, cheese, and lettuce.

3. Fold the bottom of the wrap up and over the filling. Fold in the sides and roll-up tightly, EGG ROLL-STYLE.

4. Preheat a panini or sandwich maker. Place wraps into panini maker, seam side down, and toast until wrap is crispy and toasted, 3 to 5 minutes.

5. Prepare the dip: In a small bowl, whisk together mayonnaise, vinegar, water, garlic, and sugar. Serve alongside panini wrap. (You can also add some of the dressing to the inside of the wrap.)

FROM THE PAGE TO THE PLATE

There are handy tools on each page to help you cook. Here's a quick guide.

Match the icons on these notes to the icons near the recipe. They give you added info and advice.

Learn a new cooking tip or definition while you try each recipe. "Cooking School" appears in the bottom right-hand corner of each recipe.

The highlighted word is defined or explained in "Cooking School" on the bottom right-hand corner of each recipe.

On the sample page:

Slice an avocado without the mess! First, cut it in half lengthwise. Twist the two sides to separate. Spoon out the pit. Now, you can slice the avocado into strips or cubes while holding each unpeeled half in your palm. Use a spoon to separate the avocado from the peel after slicing.

Love tomatoes? They'll also taste great in this wrap. Make sure to remove the juice and seeds first so that the juice doesn't make your wraps soggy.

COOKING SCHOOL

Once you master the "EGG ROLL-STYLE" method of folding up wraps or egg rolls, you can stuff them with all types of fillings and have a neat, perfect package you can bring anywhere. 1. Place the filling across the bottom center. 2. Fold the bottom up and over the filling. 3. Fold in the sides. 4. Roll up tightly.

HERE'S HOW!

MAKE YOUR OWN DEEP DISH PERSONAL PIZZA, LIKE WE DID (PAGE 22).

1 Grease the bottom and sides of your springform pan with nonstick cooking spray.

2 Sprinkle the bottom of the pan with cornmeal.

3 Stretch the dough to cover the bottom and 1 inch up the sides of the pan.

4 Spread sauce across the dough and top with cheese.

PENNE ROSA 16	DEEP DISH PERSONAL PIZZA 22	SPINACH QUESADILLAS 28
CREAMY ORZO 18	PANINI WRAPS 24	BROCCOLI-CHEESE BOREKAS 30
PIZZA SOUP 20	PITA PACKETS 26	PANCAKE "SANDWICHES" 32

PENNE ROSA

YIELD 6 SERVINGS

INGREDIENTS

½ cup	(1 stick) butter
1	garlic clove, crushed
1 Tbsp	flour
1	(15-oz) can tomato sauce
2 tsp	sugar
¼ tsp	salt
⅛ tsp	black pepper
1 tsp	Italian seasoning
1 cup	milk
1 lb	penne pasta, prepared according to package instructions
¼ cup	Parmesan cheese

IF you ever went out to eat in a dairy restaurant or café, you may have ordered a pasta called Penne à la Vodka, which is pasta with a pink tomato-cream sauce. I've recreated it here using no vodka or heavy cream, so it's kid-friendly and you can make it using ingredients you already have at home. Say goodbye to plain pasta with ketchup!

–L.

INSTRUCTIONS

1 Melt butter in a large SAUTÉ PAN over low heat. Add garlic. Using a wooden spoon, stir garlic until it begins to turn golden, about 2 minutes. Be careful to make sure that the garlic doesn't burn.

2 Add flour to the pan and stir. Slowly add tomato sauce to the pan and stir until smooth. Raise heat to medium. Cook for 3-4 minutes or until sauce thickens a bit. Stir in sugar, salt, pepper, and Italian seasoning.

3 Raise heat to high. Add milk and stir to combine. Let sauce cook for an additional 4 minutes, until it starts to bubble slightly. Turn off heat.

4 Add penne into the sauce a little at a time, stirring to coat the pasta in the sauce. Stir in Parmesan cheese.

 DAIRY

ITALIAN SEASONING is a mixture of dried herbs, such as basil, oregano, and thyme. It's perfect with any dish that uses tomato sauce and cheese. If you don't have the spice blend, you can use dried basil or oregano.

After you add your pasta to the boiling water, make sure to give it a stir or two so it doesn't clump together as it cooks.

COOKING SCHOOL

A **SAUTÉ PAN** is a wide pan with a flat bottom and low, straight sides. If you use a sauté pan, the sauce won't spill out of the pan, the way it might in a frying pan, which has curved sides. Your sauté pan should also come with a lid.

CREAMY ORZO

YIELD 6 SERVINGS

INGREDIENTS

- **1 Tbsp** butter
- **1½ cups** orzo
- **2** garlic cloves, crushed
- **3¾ cups** water
- **2 tsp** pareve chicken consommé powder
- **¼ cup** Parmesan cheese
- **¼ tsp** salt
- pinch coarse black pepper

SOME *people think orzo is rice. But it's actually pasta made in the shape of rice. If you like either pasta or rice (or both), then you'll love orzo.* —L.

INSTRUCTIONS

1. Melt butter in a medium saucepan over medium heat. Add orzo. Using a wooden spoon, stir orzo constantly until some pieces are golden and toasted, about 2-3 minutes.

2. Add garlic, water, and pareve chicken consommé powder. Stir. Raise heat and bring to a boil.

3. Once liquid is boiling, immediately cover pan with a lid, lower heat, and SIMMER for 20-25 minutes, until the liquid is absorbed. Turn off heat.

4. Stir in Parmesan cheese, salt, and pepper. Serve hot.

DAIRY

You can swap the Parmesan for shredded mozzarella.

This is a spork. It's a combination spoon and fork.

COOKING SCHOOL

When liquid is **SIMMERING**, you'll see little bubbles rising to the surface of the water. When liquid is boiling, the bubbles will be much larger. Most soups, sauces, and rice dishes are prepared by first bringing the liquid to a boil, and then lowering the heat and letting them simmer so that they cook gently and thoroughly.

PIZZA SOUP

YIELD 4-6 SERVINGS

INGREDIENTS

2 Tbsp	oil or butter
1	small onion, diced
1	garlic clove, minced
1	(28-oz) can crushed tomatoes
1 tsp	sugar
1 tsp	salt
1 tsp	dried basil
1 tsp	garlic powder
2 cups	milk
¼ cup	water
½ cup	shredded cheese, plus more for garnish, optional

WE love sauce and cheese, whether it's on top of our pasta or our pizza. But when do we ever get an excuse to eat it on its own?

If the picky eaters in your house don't like bits of onion in their soup, use an immersion blender to purée it before adding the cheese.

—L.

INSTRUCTIONS

1. Heat oil in a large saucepan over medium heat. Add onion and garlic. Using a wooden spoon, SAUTÉ until onion is soft, 5-7 minutes.

2. Add crushed tomatoes and cook for 8-10 minutes. Add sugar, salt, basil, garlic powder, milk, and water and stir to combine. Cook for an additional 5 minutes.

3. Add cheese. Stir until cheese is melted. Ladle soup into bowls to serve.

4. Garnish with additional shredded cheese (optional).

DAIRY

 How do you know when an onion is soft? See page 8.

 To make these cheesy pita chips, split a pita bread in half and cut it into halves or quarters. Sprinkle with shredded cheese, dried basil, and garlic powder. Bake at 425°F for 7-8 minutes, or until crispy.

COOKING SCHOOL

SAUTÉ means to cook in a hot pan with a small amount of oil. When we're sautéing, we'll use a wooden spoon to stir our ingredients occasionally so they cook evenly and don't burn. So many recipes begin with a sautéed onion — it's the first step for great flavor.

DEEP DISH PERSONAL PIZZA

YIELD 2 PERSONAL PIES

INGREDIENTS

3½ cups	flour
2 tsp	salt
2 tsp	sugar
1 tsp	active dry yeast
2 Tbsp	oil
1⅓ cup	water
1 tsp	cornmeal
1½ cups	pizza sauce
2 cups	shredded mozzarella or pizza cheese

FOR those of you who fight over the crust, this pizza is for you. You can use this same recipe to make a regular pizza pie; simply roll the dough into a 14- to 16-inch circle.

The secret to a great pizza pie is to cook it in an extra-hot oven, just like in the pizza shop. Preheat your oven so you don't waste any time.   —L.

INSTRUCTIONS

1 In a large bowl, combine flour, salt, sugar, yeast, oil, and water. Knead until smooth. Add 1 additional tablespoon of water if needed to form the mixture into a smooth dough. You can use your hands or knead the dough with an electric mixer.

2 GREASE 2 bowls with nonstick cooking spray. Divide dough in half. Shape each half into a ball and place each into a bowl. Cover with plastic wrap or a clean dish towel. Let rise for 35-40 minutes.

3 Preheat oven to 475°F. Grease two 9-inch round springform pans. Sprinkle ½ teaspoon cornmeal into each pan. Place one dough ball into the pan and stretch to cover the bottom of the pan and 1 inch up the sides of the pan. Repeat with second dough ball. See step-by-step photos on page 14.

4 Top each dough with about ¾ cup sauce and sprinkle on about 1 cup of shredded cheese. Place pizzas on the lowest rack in the oven and bake for 13-15 minutes or until cheese and crust are beginning to turn golden.

DAIRY

 See how we make this pizza step-by-step in "Here's How" on page 14.

 Baking your pizza in a metal pan (instead of a disposable) will result in a crispier crust.

Tired of pizza slices? Make pizza dip instead! Form your dough into breadsticks or "crusts." Dip them into the Pizza Soup on page 20.

COOKING SCHOOL

Very often, we **GREASE** a baking pan or baking sheet before using it so the food doesn't get stuck. "Grease" means "oil," although the easiest way to grease a pan is by spraying it with nonstick cooking spray, such as Pam.

PANINI WRAPS

YIELD 4 SERVINGS

INGREDIENTS

2	red peppers
3 Tbsp	cream cheese
4	whole wheat wraps
4 tsp	chopped fresh basil (or 4 frozen cubes, thawed)
1	avocado, sliced
4 oz	feta or mozzarella cheese
4 cups	lettuce

PANINI DIP:

¼ cup	mayonnaise
2 Tbsp	vinegar
1 Tbsp	water
1 tsp	garlic
1 tsp	sugar

WHILE we were creating recipes for this book, one mom had a request: "My teenage daughters and their friends want to know what they can prepare for lunch. They want healthy ideas that are also delicious." Well, girls, take out your panini maker, because your wraps are about to get a big upgrade. –V.

INSTRUCTIONS

1. Preheat oven to 400°F. Place whole red peppers into a baking pan and roast until the skin appears blistered (there should be some black marks all around), 35-40 minutes. Remove from oven and let cool. Once cool, the skin should peel off easily. Cut peeled peppers into four pieces. Discard seeds.

2. Spread cream cheese across the bottom-center of each wrap. Top with basil, red pepper strips, avocado, cheese, and lettuce.

3. Fold the bottom of the wrap up and over the filling. Fold in the sides and roll-up tightly, EGG ROLL-STYLE.

4. Preheat a panini or sandwich maker. Place wraps into panini maker, seam side down, and toast until wrap is crispy and toasted, 3 to 5 minutes.

5. Meanwhile, prepare the dip: In a small bowl, whisk together mayonnaise, vinegar, water, garlic, and sugar. Serve alongside panini wrap. (You can also add some of the dip to the inside of the wrap.)

 Slice an avocado without the mess! First, cut it in half lengthwise. Twist the two sides to separate. Spoon out the pit. Now, you can slice the avocado into strips or cubes while holding each unpeeled half in your palm. Use a spoon to separate the avocado from the peel after slicing.

Love tomatoes? They'll also taste great in this wrap. Make sure to remove the seeds first so that the juice doesn't make your wraps soggy.

COOKING SCHOOL

Once you master the **EGG ROLL-STYLE** method of folding up wraps or egg rolls, you can stuff them with all types of fillings and have a neat, perfect package you can take anywhere. 1. Place the filling across the bottom center. 2. Fold the bottom up and over the filling. 3. Fold in the sides. 4. Roll up tightly.

PITA PACKETS

YIELD 3 SANDWICHES

INGREDIENTS

- 1 Tbsp — oil
- 1 — onion, diced
- 4 oz — mushrooms, chopped
- 1 — garlic clove, crushed
- 3 tsp — chopped fresh basil (3 frozen basil cubes or 1 tsp dried basil)
- 1 tsp — salt
- 3 — pita breads
- ¾ cup — soft cheese (such as Tnuva or Norman's brand)

WANT

to do better than grilled cheese for lunch? These sandwiches can be wrapped up and warmed in your toaster oven. If you're making sandwiches for your younger (and picky) brothers and sisters, you can fill the sandwiches with sauce and cheese. They all still get to have fun unwrapping their own "packet."

—V.

INSTRUCTIONS

1. Preheat oven to 400°F.
2. Heat oil in a sauté pan over medium heat. Add onion. Sauté onion for 7 minutes, stirring occasionally with a wooden spoon Add mushrooms and garlic and sauté for an additional 8 minutes. Stir in basil and salt.
3. Slice off the top of each pita bread. Fill pita with the onion-mushroom mixture. Spread cheese over the onion-mushroom mixture inside the pita.
4. Wrap each sandwich tightly in a piece of aluminum foil. Bake for 10 minutes. If you want your sandwiches to be crispy, unwrap the foil and bake the sandwiches uncovered for the last few minutes.

DAIRY

> Our favorite mushrooms are baby bellas. If you're using canned mushrooms instead of fresh, they need to cook for only 3-4 minutes.

> You may have heard that you should not soak mushrooms in water to clean them because they'll absorb water like a sponge. Guess what? That's a myth! You can rinse or soak your mushrooms in water and wipe clean with a paper towel.

COOKING SCHOOL

In a rush? The smaller you chop your vegetables, the quicker they will cook. They'll also cook evenly if you chop them into evenly sized pieces.

SPINACH QUESADILLAS

YIELD 4 SERVINGS

A quesadilla, pronounced ke-sa-diya, is a flour or corn tortilla with a savory filling, including cheese. A real Mexican quesadilla is a tortilla folded into a half-moon shape. In American restaurants, two tortillas are cooked with the filling in the middle, and then cut into wedges. Any of your favorite panini or sandwich fillings can be adapted for the quesadilla — any veggies and cheese, or even guacamole with cheese will work ... have fun.

—L.

INGREDIENTS

- 2 Tbsp butter or oil
- 1 onion, finely diced
- 1 clove garlic, crushed
- 8 oz frozen spinach, thawed and drained
- ¼ cup heavy cream or milk
- ¼ cup shredded mozzarella cheese
- ¼ tsp salt, or to taste
- pinch coarse black pepper
- 8 (6-in) or 4 (10-in) flour tortillas or wraps
- 1 plum tomato, thinly sliced
- ¾ cup shredded cheddar cheese

INSTRUCTIONS

1. Heat butter or oil in a large sauté pan over medium heat. Add onion and garlic, and sauté until onion is soft, 5-7 minutes. Add spinach and cook, stirring occasionally, until spinach is cooked through, about 5 minutes. Slowly add in heavy cream or milk while stirring. Add cheese and stir to combine. Season with salt and pepper.

2. Divide spinach mixture between 4 small or 2 large wraps. Top with tomato slices and sprinkle generously with cheddar cheese. Place remaining wraps on top.

3. Heat a skillet over medium heat. Add a quesadilla. Place a pot on top of the quesadilla to weigh it down (a saucepan will work well). Cook until cheese is melted and wrap is crispy, about 5 minutes. Using a WIDE SPATULA, flip over the wrap and cook until the other side is crispy, 3-5 minutes.

DAIRY

 If you want to eat more whole wheat items, but don't think you like the taste, try a whole wheat wrap. We think they taste even better than the white flour versions.

Most varieties of tomatoes will taste better during the summer, so if you're making a tomato dish in the winter, choose plum tomatoes. They'll be the most flavorful type of tomato during the rest of the year.

COOKING SCHOOL

Having trouble flipping your wrap? When you want to flip quesadillas, pancakes, or crepes, use a **WIDE OR SLOTTED SPATULA**. They each have a wide head. A wide spatula is also the perfect type to use when you want to move sugar cookies onto a baking sheet. For more info on spatulas, see Cooking School on pages 121 and 123.

BROCCOLI-CHEESE BOREKAS

YIELD: 10 BROCCOLI & 4 CHEESE BOREKAS

INGREDIENTS

- 7 rounds malawach dough, a bit thawed
- 1 egg, beaten
- 2 Tbsp dried minced garlic or sesame seeds

BROCCOLI FILLING:
- 2 Tbsp olive oil
- 1 large onion, diced
- 1 (16-oz) bag chopped broccoli, thawed
- 1½ tsp salt
- ½ tsp garlic powder
- 3 tsp chopped fresh basil (or 3 frozen cubes)
- ¾ cup shredded cheese

CHEESE FILLING:
- 1 cup shredded cheese
- 1 egg

30 DAIRY

ALTHOUGH malawach is usually cooked in a frying pan, it also works perfectly if you want to make a really flaky boreka. Whenever I make these, I fill some of the borekas with just cheese for the kids who won't eat broccoli. —V.

INSTRUCTIONS

1. Preheat oven to 350°F. Line a baking sheet with PARCHMENT PAPER.

2. Prepare the broccoli filling: Heat oil in a sauté pan over medium-low heat. Add onion. Using a wooden spoon, sauté onion for 5 minutes. Add broccoli and sauté 15 minutes, or until soft. Stir in salt, garlic powder, and basil. Remove from heat. Let cool.

3. Stir cheese into the cooled broccoli filling.

4. Using a pizza slicer, slice each malawach circle in half. Working with one half at a time, place a spoonful of broccoli filling on one side of the dough. Fold the dough over and pinch to close. Place borekas onto prepared baking sheet.

5. When you have used all the broccoli filling, prepare the cheese filling: In a small bowl, combine cheese and egg. Fill the remaining malawach dough with the cheese filling, folding and pinching the same way. Add cheese borekas to baking sheet.

6. Brush borekas with egg and sprinkle with minced garlic or sesame seeds. Place baking sheet into oven. Bake for 25-30 minutes, or until golden brown.

Malawach dough comes with a round piece of plastic attached to each circle. It's easier to fold your borekas if you keep the dough on the plastic, and use the plastic to help you fold and pinch the dough closed. Remove the plastic before placing each boreka on the baking sheet.

You can also use puff-pastry dough instead of malawach.

COOKING SCHOOL

We like to line our baking sheets with **PARCHMENT PAPER** whenever we're baking. It's a naturally nonstick surface, so you don't need to grease it, and you can throw the paper away when you're done, making clean-up time easier. If you don't have parchment paper, line your baking sheet with aluminum foil, but spray it very well with nonstick cooking spray.

PANCAKE "SANDWICHES"

YIELD 16 PANCAKES

INGREDIENTS

1¼ cups	flour
1 Tbsp	baking powder
•	pinch salt
6 Tbsp	sugar
¼ cup	cornstarch
1	egg
1 cup	milk
1 tsp	vanilla extract
¼ cup	(½ stick) butter, melted

STRAWBERRY SYRUP:

1 cup	frozen strawberries (½ of a 16-ounce bag)
⅓ cup	sugar
2 Tbsp	water
1 tsp	vanilla extract

HOW

do you make a fun breakfast if you're not allowed to use the stove? Make pancakes in a sandwich maker. Bonus: They'll all be the same exact size. Top them with pancake syrup to completely avoid using the stove. -L.

INSTRUCTIONS

1. In a large bowl, combine flour, baking powder, salt, sugar, and cornstarch.

2. Whisk in the egg, milk, and vanilla until completely incorporated. Stir in butter.

3. Plug in a SANDWICH MAKER to preheat. When sandwich maker is hot, use a ladle to scoop up batter and pour it into each triangle. Close sandwich maker lid and cook for 4 minutes without opening. Check pancakes after 4 minutes. Cook for an additional 2 minutes for crispy pancakes.

4. Prepare the strawberry syrup: In a small saucepan, combine strawberries, sugar, water, and vanilla. Bring to a boil over high heat. Lower heat to medium-low and simmer for 15 minutes, until sauce is syrupy. Syrup will thicken more as it cools. (Optional: If you prefer a smooth, thick sauce, use a blender to purée the mixture. You may need a bit less sugar for the blended version.)

5. Drizzle syrup over pancakes. Keep refrigerated until ready to use.

DAIRY

> You can also use this batter to make pancakes or waffles on a griddle or waffle maker.

COOKING SCHOOL

SANDWICH MAKERS are convenient little cooking machines. They heat up fast and cook foods in minutes. You can use them instead of a panini maker in our Panini Wraps on page 24. (Some sandwich makers come with multiple inserts for making sandwiches, paninis, waffles, and more.) Take them along when you're going on a trip so you can enjoy hot food anywhere there's an outlet.

HERE'S HOW!

SURPRISE YOUR FAMILY WITH MINI MEAT & POTATO KNISHES (PAGE 54). HERE'S HOW WE MAKE THEM.

1 Roll out your dough. This is easiest to do if you place the dough between 2 pieces of parchment paper.

2 Cut your dough into 16 squares.

3 Place the squares on a baking sheet and spread with mustard.

4 Top with a generous spoonful of potato filling. Top with pastrami pieces.

5 Stretch the sides of the dough over the top of each knish and pinch together.

6 Flip the knishes so the seam side is down. Brush with beaten egg before baking.

HONEY BBQ CHICKEN NUGGETS 36	TACO NIGHT 44	HOT DOG GARLIC KNOTS 52
GRILLED CHICKEN STICKS 38	SINO STEAK SANDWICH 46	MEAT & POTATO KNISHES 54
CHICKEN WITH DIY BARBECUE SAUCE 40	RAMEN DELI SALAD 48	MALAFEL 56
CHICKEN OVER FRENCH FRIES 42	TERIYAKI BEEF STICKS 50	EVERYTHING FISH STICKS 58

MEAT, CHICKEN, AND FISH

HONEY BBQ CHICKEN NUGGETS

YIELD 4-6 SERVINGS

INGREDIENTS

1½ lb	chicken cutlets, cut into nuggets
2 Tbsp	oil
6 Tbsp	honey
6 Tbsp	ketchup
1 tsp	yellow mustard
½ tsp	chili powder (optional)
1½-2 cups	panko crumbs

RAISE your hand if you like dunking chicken nuggets in ketchup. What if we updated ketchup and made an even better dipping sauce for you? I like to double the sauce because my family likes to dip and dip and dip.   —L.

INSTRUCTIONS

1. Preheat oven to 375°F. Line a baking sheet with aluminum foil and spray with nonstick cooking spray.

2. In a small bowl, combine oil, honey, ketchup, mustard, and chili powder (optional). Use a spoon to stir the mixture until smooth. Pour half the sauce into a separate bowl to use as the dipping sauce; set aside.

3. Place panko CRUMBS into another bowl.

4. Dip chicken nuggets into the honey mixture and coat completely. Then, press into panko crumbs until chicken is fully coated on all sides.

5. Place chicken on prepared baking sheet. Spray the top of the nuggets with nonstick cooking spray. Bake for 25 minutes. For extra-crispy nuggets, turn the chicken halfway through the cooking time, baking for 12-13 minutes per side.

6. Serve with dipping sauce that you set aside in step 2.

MEAT, CHICKEN, & FISH

Measure the oil first. This way, when you measure the honey, it will slide right out and won't stick to the spoon. You can also spray your measuring spoon or cup with nonstick cooking spray before measuring honey.

Make sure to throw away the leftover sauce and crumbs when you have finished coating the chicken. It isn't safe to eat anything that has touched raw chicken or meat and has not been cooked.

COOKING SCHOOL

These chicken nuggets are "breaded," which means they're coated in CRUMBS. Whenever you're "breading," you'll need something sticky, like eggs or mayo, to help attach the crumbs to the chicken, fish, or veggies. For easy breading tips, see "Here's How" on page 60.

GRILLED CHICKEN STICKS

YIELD 4-6 SERVINGS

INGREDIENTS

- 1½ lb chicken cutlets, thinly sliced
- 2 Tbsp lemon juice
- 3 Tbsp oil
- 1 tsp garlic powder
- ½ tsp dried basil
- ¼ tsp salt
- ⅛ tsp black pepper
- 1 Tbsp oil, for grill pan

EQUIPMENT:
- wooden or metal skewers

NOTHING makes a mom happier than when the entire family is enjoying the same dish for dinner and there are no complaints from the picky eaters who'd prefer "something else." This so easy, so simple chicken is that "entire family pleaser." Add some 2-Potato Oven Fries (page 62) and you're set.

If you don't buy your cutlets thinly sliced, you can also simply cut them into nuggets.

-V.

INSTRUCTIONS

1. Cut chicken into thin strips and place into a medium bowl. Add lemon juice, oil, garlic powder, basil, salt, and pepper and mix to combine. Let chicken MARINATE for 30 minutes at room temperature.

2. Thread chicken onto skewers.

3. Heat 1 tablespoon oil in a grill pan over medium heat or preheat an outdoor barbecue grill. Add skewers and grill for 4-5 minutes on each side.

Love dark meat? Use boneless chicken thighs in this recipe.

If your chicken sticks to the grill or grill pan when you try to flip it, it means that the first side hasn't finished cooking. Keep cooking until it flips easily.

COOKING SCHOOL

Marinades are a mixture of liquid or spices that we add to meat before cooking. Sometimes we **MARINATE** for only a few minutes — and some recipes call for meat to be marinated for a day or two. Marinades mostly help enhance the flavor of the meat. Sometimes, they are used to tenderize it (see Cooking School on page 51). The oil in the marinade will keep your meat juicy, with the bonus of preventing it from sticking to the grill.

Chicken with DIY Barbecue Sauce

YIELD 4-6 servings

INGREDIENTS

- **1½ lb** chicken cutlets, cut into thin strips
- **2-3 Tbsp** oil

DRY BARBECUE SAUCE:
- **3 oz** (¼ cup) tomato paste OR 4-5 Tbsp ketchup
- **¼ cup** apple cider vinegar
- **2 Tbsp** brown sugar
- **2 Tbsp** honey
- **½ cup** water
- **1 Tbsp** soy sauce
- **2 tsp** garlic powder
- **1 tsp** paprika
- **1 tsp** salt
- **½ tsp** coarse black pepper

ONE of our easiest and favorite chicken dinners is simply chicken sautéed with barbecue sauce. But if you look at the back label on your bottle of barbecue sauce, you'll see that the main ingredients are tomatoes, sugar, vinegar, and spices. So why should we buy a bottle, when we can make our own sauce using ingredients we already have? Tell everyone it's your own secret sauce. –L.

INSTRUCTIONS

1. In a medium bowl, combine tomato paste, apple cider vinegar, brown sugar, honey, water, soy sauce, garlic powder, paprika, salt, and pepper. Set aside.

2. Heat oil in a sauté pan over medium heat. Add chicken to HOT oil and cook until it turns white, about 3 minutes per side.

3. Pour sauce over chicken. Cover and cook for 10-15 minutes, stirring occasionally.

Use this barbecue sauce in place of store-bought sauce in any recipe.

Serve this chicken inside a sandwich, just like we did on the cover. Toast the bun until it's crispy and add some lettuce for more crunch.

COOKING SCHOOL

When cooking chicken (or meat) in a sauté pan, make sure your oil is **HOT** before adding the chicken. You should hear a sizzling sound when you place your chicken into the pan.

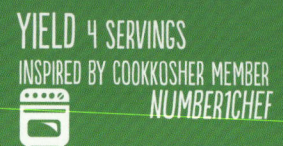

CHICKEN OVER FRENCH FRIES

YIELD 4 SERVINGS
INSPIRED BY COOKKOSHER MEMBER *NUMBER1CHEF*

INGREDIENTS

- 4 chicken pieces (or 8 drumsticks)
- 2 lb frozen French fries
- 1 tsp paprika, *divided*
- 1 tsp salt, *divided*
- 2 Tbsp oil, *divided*

HONEY-GARLIC SAUCE:

- 2 Tbsp olive oil
- 2 Tbsp honey
- 2 garlic cloves, *crushed*
- ¼ tsp black pepper

I always love to find out what the kids in other homes like to eat for dinner. One afternoon, I was speaking to a good friend and great cook, Zehava K., who was in the middle of sticking some "chicken over French fries" into the oven. I added a honey-garlic sauce and we had a new, fun version of a one-pan chicken dinner.

—L.

INSTRUCTIONS

1 Preheat oven to 400°F. Line a **BAKING SHEET** with aluminum foil and grease with nonstick cooking spray.

2 Place French fries onto the baking sheet. Sprinkle with ½ teaspoon paprika, ½ teaspoon salt, and 1 tablespoon oil. Toss the French fries until they are evenly coated with oil and spices. Spread in an even layer on the pan. Rub chicken with remaining oil and season with remaining paprika and salt. Place chicken over French fries.

3 Prepare the honey-garlic sauce: In a small bowl, combine olive oil, honey, garlic, and black pepper. Spread sauce over the chicken. Bake, uncovered, for 90 minutes. For extra-crispy chicken and fries, bake for an additional 15 minutes.

MEAT, CHICKEN, & FISH

If you don't want to use frozen fries and don't mind one extra step, cut fresh potatoes into thin French fry-shaped strips.

Although we love our fresh Oven Fries (page 62), sometimes life hands you a bag of frozen fries.

COOKING SCHOOL

We use a **BAKING SHEET** instead of a baking pan because we want our fries to be crispy. When the fries have more space on the larger baking pan, there's room for hot air to move between them and crisp up the edges. When they're crowded in a smaller baking pan, they'll steam instead of roast. The same goes when you're making any kind of roasted veggies.

TACO NIGHT

YIELD 6-8 SERVINGS

INGREDIENTS

- 2 Tbsp oil
- 2 onions, diced
- 4 garlic cloves, crushed
- 1-1½ lb ground meat
- 1½ Tbsp cumin
- ½ Tbsp paprika
- 1 Tbsp garlic powder
- pinch crushed red pepper
- ½ Tbsp salt
- 2 cups canned crushed tomatoes
- 1 ripe avocado, chopped OR 1 cup prepared guacamole
- 12 taco shells
- 2 (15-oz) cans corn, drained

TACOS are one of the most popular dinners in my house because everyone likes filling the shells with the stuff they like. Our favorite combination, though, is guacamole on the bottom of the taco shell, meat in the middle, and corn kernels on top. Although it takes just a few minutes to get the chili going, it needs to cook for awhile … that's when all the flavors develop so you get a really "wow" first bite.

—V.

INSTRUCTIONS

1. Heat oil in a **DUTCH OVEN** over medium heat. Add onions. Stirring often with a wooden spoon, sauté the onions until soft, 5-7 minutes.

2. Add garlic and meat. Using the same wooden spoon, stir meat, breaking up any large chunks. Continue until meat is mostly brown, 4-6 minutes.

3. Add cumin, paprika, garlic powder, crushed red pepper, and salt. Add crushed tomatoes. Raise heat and bring to a boil. Lower heat, cover, and simmer for 1-2 hours.

4. To serve, place a layer of avocado or guacamole into each taco shell. Fill shell with meat and top with corn.

MEAT, CHICKEN, & FISH

If you don't like big chunks of onion, mince it into small pieces in your mini chopper or food processor so it blends into the meat.

Make some Taco Chips (page 84) and use them to scoop up extra chili. The salsa on the same page makes another great taco topping.

COOKING SCHOOL

A **DUTCH OVEN** is a pot with thick sides and a lid. It's most often used in recipes where foods cook slowly over a longer period of time, like stews and roasts. If you don't have one, you can use a large saucepan or stockpot. You can also prepare steps 1 and 2 in a sauté pan, and transfer everything to a slow cooker before step 3. Cook for 4-6 hours on low.

SINO STEAK SANDWICH

YIELD 3 SANDWICHES

INGREDIENTS

- 1 lb skirt steak, cut into 5-6 pieces
- 3 Tbsp brown sugar
- 2 Tbsp honey
- 2 garlic cloves, minced
- 2 tsp vinegar
- 2 Tbsp soy sauce
- ¼ cup ketchup
- 1 Tbsp oil
- 1 onion, cut into thin strips
- 3 medium baguettes (or 1 large, cut into 3), cut open horizontally

WHEN *five boys told me they love buying Sino steak sandwiches but their mothers don't let them buy takeout as often as they want, I knew I had to help them out. The first thing I did was to go out and buy a sandwich. After all, I had to taste it myself.*

—L.

INSTRUCTIONS

1. Using a mallet, pound skirt steak on both sides.

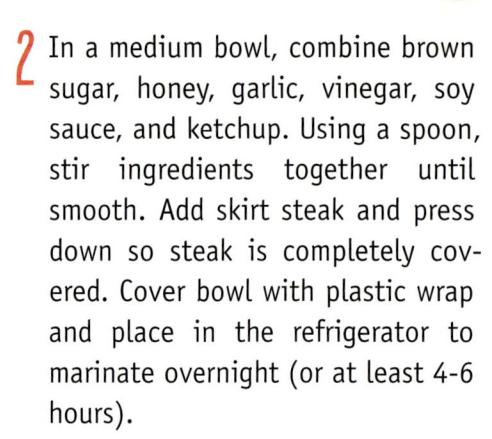

2. In a medium bowl, combine brown sugar, honey, garlic, vinegar, soy sauce, and ketchup. Using a spoon, stir ingredients together until smooth. Add skirt steak and press down so steak is completely covered. Cover bowl with plastic wrap and place in the refrigerator to marinate overnight (or at least 4-6 hours).

3. Preheat oven to 350°F. Transfer marinade and steak to a 9 x 13-inch baking pan.

4. Ask an adult to help you with this step: OVEN STEAMING. Pull out the center oven rack and place a baking pan or large roasting pan on it. The large pan must be big enough to fit your 9 x 13-inch pan inside. Pour 1 cup water into the large pan. Place the 9 x 13-inch pan with your steak and marinade into the large pan. Cover both baking pans together with aluminum foil. This "steam bath" is the trick for getting your steak soft. Bake for 1½ hours.

5. Ask an adult to pull out the rack, carefully uncover the pans,

MEAT, CHICKEN, & FISH

> Pounding the meat tenderizes it by breaking up the connective tissue. Don't have a mallet? Pound your meat with the bottom of a heavy frying pan.

> Be sure to ask an adult to put your pans into the oven and take them out when the steak is done. You can also ask an adult to cook the reserved marinade in a saucepan to create a thicker steak sauce.

COOKING SCHOOL

> It took us a lot of tries to get the texture of this meat right. Then our friend Chaya Rabinowitz, the cook behind Butterfly in Lakewood, shared a restaurant secret: the meat is steamed before being grilled. She devised this unique **OVEN STEAMING** method so we could duplicate the restaurant-quality results at home.

and remove the smaller baking pan from oven (wait until water in the larger baking pan cools before removing that pan from the oven).

6. Heat a grill or grill pan over high heat. When pan is hot, add steak and cook for 2 minutes per side. (We want to get those pretty grill marks on the steak.) Reserve the marinade.

7. Heat oil in a sauté or grill pan over medium heat (you can use the same pan). Add onion. Stirring often with a wooden spoon, sauté onion until soft, about 7 minutes.

8. Assemble the sandwiches. Place skirt steak into baguettes. Top with onions and 1-2 tablespoons of reserved marinade.

RAMEN DELI SALAD

YIELD 4 SERVINGS
INSPIRED BY COOKKOSHER MEMBER
LEA

INGREDIENTS

- 3 Tbsp vinegar
- 3 Tbsp sugar
- 3 Tbsp soy sauce
- 6 Tbsp oil
- 1 red onion, sliced
- 5 slices deli turkey breast, cut into strips
- 1 (8 oz) bag chopped Romaine lettuce
- 1 pint grape tomatoes, each cut in half

NOODLE CRUNCH:

- 1 pkg (3-oz) Ramen noodles
- ½ cup slivered almonds
- ¼ cup sesame seeds
- 1 Tbsp oil

RAMEN noodles are the ones that are included in those little packages of instant soups. We're only using the noodles themselves, not the unhealthy flavor packets that come with them. The best part of Ramen noodles is that they barely need to be cooked — and they're delicious when they're crunchy. —L.

INSTRUCTIONS

1. In a small bowl, combine vinegar, sugar, soy sauce, and oil. Use a whisk or a spoon to stir the ingredients together. Add red onion and turkey and stir to coat with the dressing. Cover bowl with plastic wrap and marinate in the refrigerator for at least 1 hour or up to overnight. This process will QUICK PICKLE the onions.

2. Prepare the noodle crunch: Preheat oven to 350°F. In a 9 x 13-inch baking pan, combine Ramen noodles, almonds, sesame seeds, and oil. Toss to combine. Bake until golden, 10-12 minutes. Set aside.

3. In a large bowl, combine lettuce, tomatoes, and turkey/dressing mixture. Toss to combine. Top with Ramen noodle mixture.

MEAT, CHICKEN, & FISH

You can make all the components of this salad in advance. The noodle crunch can be kept in an airtight container for a few days, and the turkey/dressing mixture can be kept, covered, in the refrigerator for 24 hours.

COOKING SCHOOL

The red onions in this recipe are **QUICK PICKLED**. When you soak red onions in a vinegar-based dressing, it takes the bitterness out of the raw onions while adding flavor. When you want to quick pickle any veggie, make sure to slice it thinly. For more on the classic slow pickling process, see page 91.

TERIYAKI BEEF STICKS

YIELD 8 STICKS

INGREDIENTS

- 1½ lbs sandwich steak
- ½ cup pineapple juice
- ¼ cup soy sauce
- ¼ cup honey
- 1½ tsp garlic powder

EQUIPMENT:
- 8 skewers

ANYTHING
on a stick is automatically more fun to eat. Prep these the night before or in the morning, and grill when you're ready to serve. -L.

INSTRUCTIONS

1. In a medium plastic or glass bowl, combine PINEAPPLE JUICE, soy sauce, honey, and garlic powder. Add sandwich steaks. Press down so meat is completely covered. Cover bowl with plastic wrap and refrigerate for at least 6 hours or overnight.

2. Remove steaks from marinade and thread onto skewers.

3. Grease a grill pan or sauté pan with nonstick cooking spray. Heat pan over medium-high heat. When pan is hot, add skewers and grill for 2-3 minutes per side. Serve immediately.

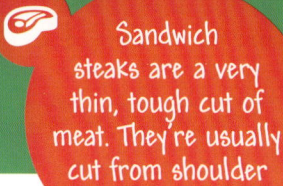

Sandwich steaks are a very thin, tough cut of meat. They're usually cut from shoulder steaks.

Tired of teriyaki? For barbecue-flavored beef sticks, use the DIY Barbecue Sauce on page 40 as a marinade. Don't forget to marinate for at least 6 hours.

We use a plastic or glass bowl in this recipe because the acid in the pineapple juice will react with metal utensils and give the mixture a metallic taste.

COOKING SCHOOL

PINEAPPLE JUICE is a powerful meat tenderizer. The enzymes in the juice break down proteins, making tough cuts of meat, like sandwich steaks, easier to eat. Don't marinate longer than a day or the meat will turn mushy. For more info on marinades, see Cooking School on page 38.

HOT DOG GARLIC KNOTS

YIELD 36 KNOTS

INGREDIENTS

1¾ cup	flour
1 tsp	salt
1 tsp	sugar
½ tsp	active dry yeast
1 Tbsp	oil
⅔ cup	water
6	hot dogs, each cut into 6 pieces
2 Tbsp	olive oil
2 tsp	garlic powder
2 tsp	parsley flakes
•	pinch salt

WHAT

do you do to please the neighborhood boys? You combine two of their favorite foods: hot dogs and garlic knots.

—L.

INSTRUCTIONS

1. In a large bowl, combine flour, salt, sugar, yeast, oil, and water. Knead until smooth. Add 1 additional tablespoon of water if necessary. You can use your hands or knead the dough with an electric mixer.

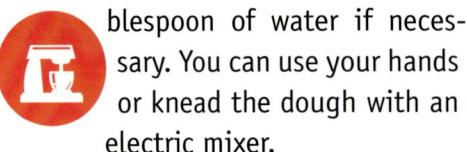

2. Grease a bowl with nonstick cooking spray. Place dough in bowl, cover with plastic wrap or a clean towel, and let RISE for 35-40 minutes. You can keep it in the mixer bowl or place it in a separate bowl.

3. Preheat oven to 425°F. Line a baking sheet with parchment paper.

4. Divide dough into 4 parts. Cut each part into 9 pieces. Stretch each piece into a rectangle and wrap it around a piece of hot dog. Tie a knot at the top, and tuck the two ends underneath. You can also simply wrap the dough around the hot dog. Place wrapped hot dogs on prepared baking sheet. Bake for 18-22 minutes until golden brown.

5. Meanwhile, in a large bowl, combine olive oil, garlic powder, parsley, and salt. Toss hot dogs in garlic mixture as soon as they come out of the oven.

MEAT, CHICKEN, & FISH

To save a step, you can use store-bought dough or take a piece of your mom's challah dough to wrap up your hot dogs. You can also save some of your pizza dough or the pretzel dough from the Hot Pretzels on page 78.

COOKING SCHOOL

Most dough that contains yeast needs to RISE before it is baked. Place your dough into a large greased bowl in a warm spot in your kitchen. You should cover it with plastic wrap or a clean dish towel so it doesn't form a crust. You'll see the dough growing bigger and bigger as the yeast creates air bubbles inside it. Be patient!

MEAT AND POTATO KNISHES

YIELD 18 KNISHES

INGREDIENTS

- 5 Yukon Gold potatoes, peeled and cut into chunks
- 1 egg

DOUGH:
- ¼ cup oil
- 2¾ cups flour
- 1 tsp baking powder
- 2 tsp salt
- 1 cup water

FILLING:
- 3 Tbsp oil
- 1 large onion, chopped
- 2 tsp salt
- ⅓ cup favorite mustard
- 4 oz sliced pastrami or corned beef, cut into small squares

THERE used to be a restaurant in town that made the best mini knishes. Whenever I'd go there, I'd only order knishes and coleslaw, and that would be my dinner. Now I make them myself.

—V.

INSTRUCTIONS

1. Place potatoes into a large pot and cover with water. Place pot over high heat and bring water to a boil. Boil until potatoes are soft, about 20 minutes. Ask an adult to drain the potatoes in a colander.

2. In a bowl, mash the potatoes.

3. Preheat oven to 350°F. Line a baking sheet with parchment paper.

4. Prepare the dough: In a large bowl, combine 1 cup mashed potatoes, oil, flour, baking powder, salt, and water. First, use a spoon and mix until ingredients are combined. Then, knead dough with your hands until smooth. Set aside.

5. Prepare the filling: Heat oil in a sauté pan over medium heat. Add onion and sauté until completely soft and slightly golden, about 10 minutes. In a medium bowl, combine remaining mashed potatoes, sautéed onion, and salt.

6. On a piece of parchment paper, roll out dough to ¼-inch thick (if you can't roll the dough thin enough, you can always stretch out the dough after cutting into squares). Cut the dough into 3-inch squares. See step-by-step photos on page 34.

7. Spread squares with mustard. Place a large spoonful of potato filling on

MEAT, CHICKEN, & FISH

mustard. Top with two squares of pastrami. (The knishes will double in size while baking, so you want them to be really stuffed.)

8. Stretch the sides of the dough over the top of the knish and pinch together. Place on prepared baking sheet, seam side down.

9. Prepare the EGG WASH: Break egg into a bowl. Using a fork, beat the egg. Using a pastry brush, brush knishes with beaten egg.

10. Place baking sheet into oven. Bake until knishes are golden, 25-30 minutes.

Regular mustard is made from mustard seeds mixed with other ingredients and then blended until smooth. Whole grain mustard, used here, is mustard before it's been blended.

See how we create these knishes step-by-step in "Here's How" on page 34.

If you're not a deli fan, you'll love these knishes with ground meat instead. You'll have to brown the meat with a little bit of oil in a frying pan and add a pinch of salt. Use it instead of pastrami in step 7.

COOKING SCHOOL

An EGG WASH is made from a beaten egg, sometimes mixed with other ingredients, like water or sugar. We brush egg on the raw dough so that it turns golden and shiny while baking.

MALAFEL

YIELD 4 servings

INGREDIENTS

- 1 lb ground beef
- 1 garlic clove, crushed
- 1 tsp salt
- 2 tsp cumin
- 1 tsp ground coriander
- 1 tsp onion powder
- 2 Tbsp oil
- 4 pita breads, tops cut off
- ¼ cup hummus
- 1 cup Israeli salad OR diced cucumbers and tomatoes
- 1 cup red cabbage OR our favorite "purple salad" (see note)
- ¼ cup techineh

As a huge falafel fan, I set out to create a meat dinner while still getting my falafel fix.

My taste-testers, the neighborhood boys, all shocked me by filling their pitas with the meat and tons of salad and requesting seconds. They left the house and sat outside in the shade arguing about what to call my creation. Their choice? "Eata meata pita."

—L.

INSTRUCTIONS

1. In a small bowl, gently combine meat, garlic, salt, cumin, coriander, and onion powder. You can refrigerate the meat or freeze it until ready to cook.

2. Heat oil in a skillet or sauté pan over medium-high heat. Form the meat mixture into little balls like falafel balls, or simply place the entire mixture into the hot oil. Use a wooden spoon to break the meat into pieces as it cooks. BROWN the meat, cooking until it is brown on all sides, about 10 minutes, stirring occasionally.

3. Spread 1 tablespoon hummus inside each pita bread. Fill with meat, Israeli salad, and red cabbage. Top with techineh.

MEAT, CHICKEN, & FISH

Do you want to make techineh? Blend ½ cup tahini paste, juice of 2 lemons (about 5-6 Tbsp), ⅓ cup water, 1 tsp salt, and 3 garlic cloves.

Purple Salad

3 Tbsp vinegar
½ tsp sugar
½ tsp salt
pinch black pepper
1-2 tsp oil
1 (8-oz) bag shredded purple cabbage
½ small red onion, thinly sliced
2-3 Tbsp toasted sesame seeds

In a small bowl, combine the vinegar, sugar, salt, pepper, and oil. In a large mixing bowl, combine cabbage, onion, and sesame seeds. Toss with dressing just before serving.

COOKING SCHOOL

To **BROWN** your meat and get the best flavor, the oil must first be very hot or the meat will stick. We also use this cooking technique in our Tacos (page 44).

EVERYTHING FISH STICKS

YIELD 20 STICKS

INGREDIENTS

- ½ cup mayonnaise
- 3 Tbsp honey
- ¾ cup cornflake crumbs
- ¼ cup cornmeal
- 3 Tbsp sesame seeds
- 2 Tbsp poppy seeds
- 2 Tbsp dried minced onion
- 2 Tbsp dried minced garlic
- ¾ Tbsp sea salt
- 1 lb flounder or tilapia, cut into nuggets or sticks

LOTS of kids like fish sticks … and many more kids love an everything bagel. So, we gave fish sticks a very tasty upgrade that will save you a trip to the bagel store.

–V.

INSTRUCTIONS

1. Preheat oven to 400°F. Line a baking sheet with parchment paper.

2. In a small bowl, combine mayonnaise and honey. In a second small bowl, combine CORNFLAKE CRUMBS, cornmeal, sesame seeds, poppy seeds, minced onion, minced garlic, and sea salt.

3. Pour about half the cornflake mixture into a shallow dish or plate. Add more cornflake mixture as you use it up.

4. Coat tilapia nuggets in mayonnaise mixture, then coat with cornflake mixture. Place on prepared baking sheet and spray with nonstick cooking spray. Bake until nuggets are golden, about 20 to 25 minutes. For extra crispiness, bake an additional 5-10 minutes. Optional: Serve with tartar sauce. (Make your own! See note.) See step-by-step photos on page 60.

58 MEAT, CHICKEN, & FISH

Don't use your fingers to coat the fish sticks in crumbs. Use the same method that we used when breading the Cauliflower Poppers. See "Here's How" on page 60.

You can make your own tartar sauce by combining

¼ cup mayonnaise

1 Tbsp sweet pickle relish

1 tsp lemon juice

pinch each of parsley, salt, and pepper

Or, enjoy these with the Honey Mustard Dip on page 72.

COOKING SCHOOL

We used **CORNFLAKE CRUMBS** to coat these fish sticks. Other ingredients you can use to give foods a crispy coating include bread crumbs, as in our Cauliflower Poppers on page 72, or panko crumbs, as in our Honey BBQ Chicken Nuggets on page 36.

HERE'S HOW! MAKE PERFECT CAULIFLOWER POPPERS (PAGE 72) WITHOUT MAKING A MESS.

1 Make sure your cauliflower is dry.

2 First, coat your cauliflower in flour. Work with a few florets at a time. Shake off the extra flour.

3 Drop your cauliflower into the egg. Use your fingers to turn the cauliflower around to coat completely. Let the extra egg drip down into the plate.

4 Place your cauliflower into the dish with the breadcrumbs. Using a spoon, spoon some breadcrumbs over the top of the cauliflower. (Don't use your fingers, or the egg on your fingers will make the breadcrumbs clumpy.)

5 Place the coated cauliflower on a greased baking sheet and spray with nonstick cooking spray.

2-POTATO OVEN FRIES 62	PEACH & MANGO SALAD 66	SUGAR SNAP PEAS & EDAMAME 70
ROASTED DIJON POTATOES 64	VEGGIE STICKS WITH RED PEPPER DIP 68	CAULIFLOWER POPPERS 72
		ZUCCHINI SPAGHETTI 74

ON THE SIDE

2-POTATO OVEN FRIES

YIELD 4-6 SERVINGS
INSPIRED BY COOKKOSHER MEMBER CS

INGREDIENTS

- 2 sweet potatoes, cut into French fry sticks
- 2 Yukon Gold potatoes, cut into French fry sticks
- 1½ tsp kosher salt
- 1 tsp garlic powder
- 1 tsp cumin
- ¼ tsp ground black pepper
- ¼ cup oil

ONCE you gain more experience cooking, you'll learn how it's possible to change each recipe to make it your own. This recipe, though, has a funny personality. It's only perfect when you use this exact amount of oil and spices. Whenever we tried to make it without measuring, it wasn't the same! If you love falafel or falafel-flavored snacks like Bissli, then you like cumin. These will be the only fries you love better than the fries in the pizza shop.

—L.

INSTRUCTIONS

1. Preheat oven to 425°F. Line two baking sheets with parchment paper, or line with aluminum foil and grease with nonstick cooking spray.

2. In a large bowl, combine both kinds of POTATOES, salt, garlic powder, cumin, pepper, and oil. Toss to combine so oil and spices are evenly distributed.

3. Spread potatoes in an even layer on the baking sheets. Bake for 45 minutes or until crispy.

ON THE SIDE

You can skip the bowl and toss your French fries right on the baking sheet (less clean up!).

Sweet potatoes are usually larger than Yukon Gold potatoes. If you are using only sweet potatoes, you'll need 3. If you are using only Yukon Gold potatoes, you'll need 5-6.

COOKING SCHOOL

What kind of POTATOES are the best for French fries? We like the taste of Yukon Gold potatoes best. They are also called "yellow" potatoes or "butter" potatoes. Russets, though, are the classic "French fry" potato.

ROASTED DIJON POTATOES

YIELD 4-6 SERVINGS
INSPIRED BY COOKKOSHER MEMBER *RABASH*

INGREDIENTS

- 2 lb red potatoes, cut into wedges
- 2 Tbsp mayonnaise
- 2 Tbsp Dijon mustard
- 2 Tbsp oil
- 1½ tsp salt
- pinch coarse black pepper

EVERY cook needs a good roasted potato in his or her repertoire. We love these because the mayonnaise helps all the flavoring stick to the potatoes, resulting in an extra crispy crust.

—V.

INSTRUCTIONS

1. Preheat oven to 350°F.
2. Place potatoes into a 9 x 13-inch baking pan and toss with mayonnaise, MUSTARD, oil, salt, and pepper.
3. Bake until crispy, 50-60 minutes. Stir the potatoes halfway through the baking time.

ON THE SIDE

Two pounds of potatoes equals about 5 or 6 medium potatoes.

COOKING SCHOOL

All **MUSTARDS** are made from mustard seeds, but they are mixed with different ingredients for different flavors. Dijon mustard is made with white wine, while yellow mustard gets its color from turmeric. Spicy brown mustard has more spices and is coarsely ground, which is why it looks speckled.

PEACH AND MANGO SALAD

YIELD 4 SERVINGS

INGREDIENTS

1	(8-oz) bag chopped Romaine lettuce
1	peach, sliced
1	mango, diced
3 Tbsp	dried cranberries
¼ cup	salted peanuts

DRESSING:

1½ Tbsp	lemon juice
1½ Tbsp	sugar
¾ tsp	salt
•	pinch coarse black pepper
3 Tbsp	oil

IF *you want to learn how to make a great salad using whatever ingredients you have in the house, here are my rules: 1) I like something crunchy (like nuts or croutons, or a really crunchy veggie like carrots). 2) I like something chewy (dried cranberries do the job here). 3) I like when I taste salty and sweet together in one bite, like I do in this salad.*

—L.

INSTRUCTIONS

1. In a large bowl, combine lettuce, peach, mango, dried cranberries, and peanuts.

2. Prepare the DRESSING: In a small bowl, combine lemon juice, sugar, salt, pepper, and oil. Stir together with a whisk or a spoon.

3. Drizzle dressing over salad and toss to combine.

Choose ripe peaches and mangoes. If they're too hard, they will not be sweet. Too mushy isn't good either (although great for a smoothie). The fruit should be a little soft and give just a bit when you press on the skin.

During the winter, when peaches aren't in season, use two mangoes.

COOKING SCHOOL

A good basic salad DRESSING always contains an acid (like vinegar or lemon juice), spices, and oil. Whisk the acid with the salt and sugar first so they dissolve. Add in the rest of your ingredients, but drizzle in the oil last and whisk again to combine.

VEGGIE STICKS with RED PEPPER DIP

YIELD SCANT ¾ CUP DIP

INGREDIENTS

- ½ small red bell pepper
- ½ cup mayonnaise
- 2 tsp vinegar
- 2 tsp sugar
- 1 garlic clove
- ½ tsp salt
- 1 Tbsp water, if needed
- assorted vegetables (such as carrots, cucumbers, celery, kohlrabi, and peppers), cut into sticks

ONE day, my neighbor knocked on my door with a container of her son's favorite store-bought dip. She had a request. Could I please figure out the recipe so that she could make it herself instead of spending $3.99 for each small container?

I got right to work. Half an hour later, I delivered a container of dip for my neighbor's family to taste. Now they're dipping away.

—L.

INSTRUCTIONS

1. In the bowl of a mini chopper or FOOD PROCESSOR, combine pepper, mayonnaise, vinegar, sugar, garlic, and salt. Blend until smooth. Whisk in water, if necessary, to thin the dip to desired consistency.

2. Serve dip alongside veggie sticks.

ON THE SIDE

If you want to use an immersion blender to make this dip, ask an adult for help. We don't recommend that kids use it on their own. Chop the red pepper into smaller pieces before blending.

COOKING SCHOOL

BLENDERS and **FOOD PROCESSORS** perform very different jobs. Use a blender when you want to turn a mixture into a liquid. It will make a soup or a smoothie much smoother and more velvety. It can also crush ice, while a food processor usually can't. Food processors are better for chopping and mincing. Chop your nuts or veggies in the food processor, or grate veggies, cheese, or potatoes. A "mini chopper" is a smaller, more convenient version of a food processor. You can use any of these appliances to make a dip like this one.

SUGAR SNAP PEAS AND EDAMAME

YIELD 6 SERVINGS

INGREDIENTS

- 1½ lb sugar snap peas
- 1 cup shelled edamame
- 1 Tbsp oil
- 1½ tsp salt
- 1½ tsp dried minced onion

LAST summer, my family went to a vegetable farm so we could pick our own sugar snap peas. That's how I ended up with loads of them and discovered the absolute best way to cook these crunchy pods. You don't need to boil water or take out a sauté pan to get the best flavor out of a sugar snap pea. They're perfect in just a few minutes of roasting time in the oven. Especially in the summertime, sugar snap peas are sweet like their name and don't need anything else.

–V.

INSTRUCTIONS

1. Preheat oven to 450°F. Line a baking sheet with parchment paper.

2. Place sugar snap peas and edamame on the baking sheet. Drizzle with oil and season with salt and minced onion. Toss vegetables until the oil and spices are evenly distributed. Spread the peas and beans into an even layer on the baking sheet.

3. ROAST in the oven for 10 minutes.

Edamame is the soybean in the pod. The pod is tough and not really edible. You can buy them already shelled (without the pod) for this recipe. But, just like peanuts in the shell or sunflower seeds, they're fun to eat with the pod too. Boil or microwave the pods, sprinkle with some sea salt, and bite the pod off as you eat.

This recipe will work perfectly with lots of "green" things, such as green beans, spring peas, or asparagus.

COOKING SCHOOL

These veggies are roasted. Roasting means cooking food, uncovered, at a very high temperature and without a liquid. We usually ROAST in an oven, although roasting can also be done over an open fire (like when you roast your hot dogs at a campfire).

CAULIFLOWER POPPERS

YIELD 4-6 SERVINGS

INGREDIENTS

- 1 (24-oz) bag frozen cauliflower, THAWED
- ½ cup flour
- 3 eggs
- 1 cup seasoned breadcrumbs

HONEY MUSTARD DIP:
- 3 Tbsp mayonnaise
- 1 Tbsp honey
- 2 tsp mustard
- ¼ tsp salt
- pinch coarse black pepper
- ⅛ tsp dried dill

THIS is the vegetable version of chicken nuggets. Some sneaky moms purée cauliflower and mix it into mac-n-cheese to get their kids to eat vegetables. No need for that! After trying these, kids will love cauliflower on its own merit. –V.

INSTRUCTIONS

1. Preheat oven to 425°F. Grease a baking sheet with nonstick cooking spray.

2. Dry the cauliflower florets with a paper towel.

3. Prepare 3 shallow bowls. Place flour into the first bowl, crack the eggs into the second bowl, and pour breadcrumbs into the third bowl. With a fork, lightly beat the eggs.

4. Work with a few florets at a time. Toss cauliflower in flour to coat. Shake off any extra. Then, drop cauliflower in the egg. Use your fingers to turn the cauliflower to coat it completely. Let any extra egg drip back into the bowl. See step-by-step photos on page 60.

5. Drop the cauliflower into the breadcrumbs. Spoon breadcrumbs over the florets to coat completely. Place florets, spread apart, on prepared baking sheet. Spray generously with nonstick cooking spray. Bake for 35 minutes, or until golden and crispy.

6. Prepare the honey mustard dip: In a small bowl, combine mayonnaise, honey, mustard, salt, pepper, and dill. Using a spoon, stir together until smooth. Drizzle over baked Cauliflower Poppers or use as a dip.

ON THE SIDE

🔍 To see how we coat our cauliflower step-by-step, see "Here's How" on page 60.

If your cauliflower is frozen and you don't want to wait for it to thaw, place it in a microwave-safe bowl and microwave for about 3 minutes, or until it is no longer cold.

COOKING SCHOOL

You can **THAW** — defrost — most frozen foods by moving them from the freezer to the refrigerator the day before you want to use them (just don't thaw the ice cream!). Dough and veggies will thaw in a few minutes to a couple of hours on the counter at room temperature. It's best to put frozen liquids (such as milk or non-dairy whipped topping) and frozen meat or chicken into a bowl of cold water to thaw on the counter.

ZUCCHINI SPAGHETTI

YIELD 4-6 servings

INGREDIENTS

- **3 Tbsp** oil, divided
- **1** garlic clove, crushed
- **½ cup** breadcrumbs
- **3** zucchinis, JULIENNED or grated
- **¼ tsp** salt
- pinch coarse black pepper
- **2 tsp** lemon juice

THIS *has to be the most satisfying and fun way to eat zucchini. Twirl it around with your fork and enjoy the crunch.*

—V.

INSTRUCTIONS

1 Heat 2 tablespoons oil in a sauté pan over medium heat. Add garlic and stir for 1 minute. Add breadcrumbs. Using a wooden spoon, stir constantly until breadcrumbs are golden and toasted, 2-3 minutes. Remove breadcrumbs from pan.

2 Add remaining 1 tablespoon oil to the pan. Add zucchini and sauté for 3 minutes. Stir in salt, pepper, lemon juice, and toasted breadcrumbs.

ON THE SIDE

You can make this dish more colorful by using a yellow squash instead of one of the zucchinis. Carrots and beets can also be julienned into pretty strips.

You won't be able to use the seed-filled centers of the zucchini when julienning. What to do with them? Sauté an onion in a bit of oil, add the chopped zucchini centers, and continue to sauté until soft. Season with salt and pepper.

COOKING SCHOOL

JULIENNE means to cut into thin strips. We use a special julienne peeler to make this job easy. It looks just like a regular vegetable peeler, but it has little teeth in the blade. For easy julienning, place a vegetable on a cutting board. Stick a fork into one side to hold the vegetable in place while you run the julienne peeler down the side of the vegetable.

HERE'S HOW!

HERE'S HOW TO TWIST A PRETZEL TO CREATE OUR HOT PRETZELS (PAGE 78).

1 Begin by dividing the dough into 8 balls.

2 Roll each ball into a thin, long rope, between 26 and 28 inches in length.

3 Create a loop by folding one end of the rope over the other.

4 Fold the bottom rope over the top to create a twist.

5 Fold the two ropes up and pinch them against the top of the loop.

6 Dip the pretzel into the baking powder/water mixture and place on a baking sheet.

7 Brush with butter immediately after baking.

HOT PRETZELS 78	TACO CHIPS & SALSA 84	HOT BANANA PEPPERS 90
ONION N' GARLIC POPCORN 80	GRAB & GO MUFFINS 86	SKINNY BERRY COOLATA 92
TOASTED BOW-TIE CHIPS 82	CHEWY PB GRANOLA BARS 88	ICED VANILLA 93

SNACK TIME

HOT PRETZELS

YIELD 8 PRETZELS
INSPIRED BY COOKKOSHER MEMBER *FROSTING*

INGREDIENTS

DOUGH:
- **3 tsp** instant dry yeast
- **1½ cups** warm water
- **2 Tbsp** sugar
- **4 cups** flour
- **1 tsp** salt

CRUST:
- **1 cup** water
- **2 tsp** baking powder
- coarse sea salt or kosher salt
- **¼ cup** (½ stick) butter or margarine, melted

WHEN I was a kid, I walked to school. On my way, I'd stop to buy a hot pretzel for 50¢ to eat instead of school lunch. If you want to take these to school, freeze in individual bags right after they cool. Grab one in the morning, and when lunchtime rolls around, the pretzel will be ready to eat. —L.

INSTRUCTIONS

1. In a large bowl, combine YEAST, warm water, and sugar. Add in flour and salt and knead until smooth. You can use your hands or knead the dough with an electric mixer.

2. Grease a second bowl with nonstick cooking spray and place dough into the bowl. Cover with plastic wrap or a clean dish towel and let rise for 30 minutes.

3. Preheat oven to 425°F. Line 2 baking sheets with parchment paper.

4. Divide dough into 8 equal parts. Roll each part into a rope about 26-28 inches long and form into a pretzel shape. See step-by-step photos on page 76.

5. In a shallow bowl, combine water and baking powder. Place pretzels, one at a time, into the water. Pretzel should be completely under the water. Remove from bowl and place onto prepared baking sheets. Sprinkle with salt. Let pretzels rest for 5-10 minutes.

6. Bake for 12-15 minutes, until golden brown.

7. Brush melted butter onto hot pretzels immediately after taking them out of the oven.

78 SNACK TIME

Making pretzels is a great rainy day activity. For easier shaping, you can make pretzel rods instead of twisted pretzels.

See "Here's How" on page 76 to learn the best way to twist a pretzel.

The baking powder bath gives the pretzels their texture and shiny brown crust.

COOKING SCHOOL

We like to use **INSTANT DRY YEAST** instead of fresh yeast because it's more practical. It's easy to measure and is inexpensive when you buy it in the bag. After you open the bag, keep your yeast in an airtight container in the fridge or freezer and it will last for awhile. 6¾ teaspoons dry yeast = 2 ounces fresh yeast.

ONION n' GARLIC POPCORN

YIELD 1 SERVING
INSPIRED BY COOKKOSHER MEMBER BUCBUC20

INGREDIENTS

- **3 Tbsp** popcorn kernels
- **¼ tsp** fine table salt
- **½ tsp** onion powder
- **½ tsp** garlic powder
- nonstick cooking spray

EQUIPMENT:
- **1** brown paper bag

IF you knew how easy it is to pop your own popcorn in the microwave, you'd never buy bags of microwave popcorn, or buy the popcorn already popped, or even pop popcorn in a pot! But you would make sure to always have brown paper bags on hand. Don't forget to decorate your bags before popping, like we did. —L.

INSTRUCTIONS

1. Place the popcorn kernels into a brown paper bag. Fold over the top of the bag two or three times.

2. Lay the bag flat in the MICROWAVE. Microwave for 90 seconds. If you don't hear your kernels popping, your microwave may need an extra minute. Don't open the microwave right away when the time is up. Wait until you hear the kernels stop popping.

3. Wait for a minute or two before opening bag. Pour popcorn into a large bowl. Season with salt.

4. To flavor the popcorn: Spray popcorn with nonstick cooking spray (this will help make the flavors stick) and sprinkle with onion powder and garlic powder. Toss popcorn in the bowl so the flavors are evenly distributed.

SNACK TIME

For barbecue-flavored popcorn, use the same spices we use on the Barbecue Bow-Tie Chips on page 82.

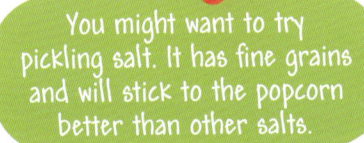

You might want to try pickling salt. It has fine grains and will stick to the popcorn better than other salts.

COOKING SCHOOL

MICROWAVE OVENS are very useful for rapidly heating or cooking foods — but be careful. If you're microwaving any closed container, steam can get trapped inside, just like when making this popcorn. Wait a couple of minutes before opening the container.

TOASTED BOW-TIE CHIPS

YIELD 5½ CUPS

INGREDIENTS

1 lb	bow-tie pasta
3 Tbsp	oil
2 tsp	salt
	BARBECUE BOW-TIES:
1 tsp	chili powder
1 tsp	paprika
1 tsp	sugar
1 tsp	garlic powder
	SEA SALT BOW-TIES:
2 tsp	kosher or sea salt

DO you fight over the crispy tops and edges of baked ziti or macaroni and cheese? Then this is a crunchy snack you'll love. You can have them plain with salt (because lots of us like plain noodles) or make barbecue chips.
—V.

INSTRUCTIONS

1. Prepare PASTA according to package instructions. Drain and return pasta to the pot. Add in oil and salt. Using a wooden spoon, stir to combine.

2. Preheat oven to 350°F. Line 2 baking sheets with parchment paper.

3. Spread bow-ties in a single layer on prepared baking sheets. (You will have a little pasta left over. You can bake the rest when the first batch is done.)

4. Bake until bow-ties are golden, about 30-35 minutes. Bow-ties will bake faster when the tray isn't full, so check them after 25 minutes if you're making a smaller batch.

5. For barbecue bow-ties: In a small bowl, combine chili powder, paprika, sugar, and garlic powder.

6. As soon as they come out of the oven, toss hot crunchy bow-ties with barbecue seasoning or salt in a large bowl.

SNACK TIME

These bow-ties can also be deep-fried instead of baked.

COOKING SCHOOL

To keep **PASTA** from clumping together during cooking, make sure you use plenty of water. Pasta needs space to cook evenly and avoid sticking together. Don't forget to stir a couple of times after adding the pasta to the pot.

TACO CHIPS AND SALSA

YIELD 40 CHIPS & 2 CUPS SALSA

INGREDIENTS

TACOS:
- 5 (10-in) wraps
- ¼ tsp salt
- ¼ tsp garlic powder
- ¼ tsp paprika
- ¼ tsp chili powder

SALSA:
- 1 Tbsp oil
- ½ onion, finely diced
- 1 garlic clove, crushed
- 1 (15-oz) can diced tomatoes
- ½ tsp salt
- pinch crushed red pepper
- 1 tsp chopped fresh parsley, optional

WHAT did we do when we didn't like the dinner served at summer camp? My bunkmates and I pulled out a bag of taco chips and salsa, no plates or cutlery needed. Here's the homemade version of that summer memory. Even when you do like dinner, chips and salsa are a great snack or appetizer. —L.

INSTRUCTIONS

1. Preheat oven to 375°F. Line a baking sheet with parchment paper.

2. Using a pizza slicer, slice each wrap in half. Slice in half again, and again, until you have 8 triangles (like a pizza). Place triangles on the baking sheet. Spray very well with nonstick cooking spray and sprinkle with salt, garlic powder, paprika, and chili powder. Bake for 7-8 minutes, until crispy and golden brown on the edges.

3. Prepare the salsa: Heat oil in a sauté pan over medium heat. Add onion and garlic. Stirring occasionally with a wooden spoon, sauté onion until golden, about 12 minutes.

4. Pour the diced TOMATOES into a strainer to drain the liquid. Add the tomatoes to the pan and cook, stirring occasionally, for 5 minutes. Season with salt, crushed red pepper, and optional parsley. Keep in the refrigerator until ready for dipping.

SNACK TIME

If you like your salsa hot, a bit of diced jalapeño pepper will do the trick, but let an adult do the chopping for you. If you touch your eyes after touching the seeds, they can really burn.

COOKING SCHOOL

TOMATOES straight out the can taste a little bitter. That's because they are high in acid, which helps preserve them. When you cook the tomatoes or tomato sauce, the bitterness goes away.

GRAB AND GO MUFFINS

YIELD 12 MUFFINS
INSPIRED BY COOKKOSHER MEMBER LUV2COOK

INGREDIENTS

1½ cups	whole wheat flour
1 cup	quick cooking oats
¾ cup	brown sugar
1½ tsp	baking soda
2 tsp	baking powder
1	egg
2 Tbsp	oil
1 cup	orange juice
1 tsp	vanilla extract
½ cup	chocolate chips

WE tested lots of low-fat whole wheat muffins to find the ones that kids and teens would really want to eat. These are the winner! If you want to keep some in the freezer to grab when there's no time for breakfast (just warm them in the microwave for a few seconds), then make sure that no one is around when you take them out of the oven. The tops of these muffins get that crispiness that everyone loves.

–V.

INSTRUCTIONS

1. Preheat oven to 350ºF. Line a 12-cup muffin pan with cupcake liners.

2. In a large bowl, combine flour, oats, brown sugar, BAKING SODA, and BAKING POWDER. Using a fork, mix well.

3. Add in egg, oil, orange juice, and vanilla. Using a large spoon, mix until all ingredients are combined. Stir in chocolate chips. Using a large spoon, drop batter into each muffin cup, filling it almost to the top.

4. Bake for 30 minutes.

If you don't have cupcake liners, just spray your muffin pan very well with nonstick cooking spray. Hold your pan over the sink so the spray doesn't spritz all over.

COOKING SCHOOL

Both **BAKING SODA** and **BAKING POWDER** are made from sodium bicarbonate, which will make your muffins rise. Baking soda is more powerful, but too much can make your batter taste bitter. Baking powder has a more neutral taste (from the other ingredients that are added to it), so it can finish the job without affecting the flavor.

CHEWY PB GRANOLA BARS

YIELD 12 BARS

INGREDIENTS

- *2 cups* quick cooking oats
- *2 Tbsp* oil
- *⅓ cup* honey
- *½ cup* peanut butter
- *½ cup* Rice Krispies
- *¼ cup* whole wheat flour
- *¼ cup* chocolate chips

IN the supermarket, granola bars come in two different versions: crunchy and chewy. They both work as an energizing snack or treat. I used to think the crunchy versions were my favorite. Now, I'm not so sure. –V.

INSTRUCTIONS

1. Preheat oven to 350°F. Line a baking sheet with parchment paper.

2. Add OATS to the prepared baking sheet. Drizzle oil on top and toss to combine. Spread oats in an even layer and bake for 5 minutes.

3. In a medium bowl, combine honey and peanut butter. Microwave for 20 seconds. Stir in oats, Rice Krispies, flour, and chocolate chips (these should be added last so they don't melt).

4. Spread mixture into a 9 x 5-inch loaf baking pan. Refrigerate until completely cooled. Cut into bars.

You can add any chopped nuts to your granola bar.

COOKING SCHOOL

You'll see both old-fashioned OATS and quick cooking oats on your grocery store shelf. They're both made from the same oats. Quick cooking oats are simply chopped into smaller pieces so they cook more quickly.

HOT BANANA PEPPERS

YIELD 2 POUNDS

INGREDIENTS

¾ lb	banana or yellow wax peppers
6	garlic cloves
1¾ cup	water
2 Tbsp	salt
½ cup	vinegar

EQUIPMENT

1	quart-sized Mason jar

ONE of my daughter's teachers instituted a new school rule: The girls are not allowed to bring hot banana peppers to school. They all used to bring these peppers in their small plastic containers for snack. The juices would drip everywhere and the teacher didn't like the smell. I don't understand how those girls can eat dozens and dozens of hot burning peppers, but since they love them, let them make them fresh. As long as there is plenty of water to drink nearby. —L.

INSTRUCTIONS

1. Wearing plastic gloves, cut peppers into rings and pop out the ribs and seeds. Add pepper rings and garlic into the Mason jar.

2. Prepare the BRINE: In a measuring cup, combine water and salt. Pour over pepper rings in the jar. Add vinegar to jar.

3. Seal jar and shake well.

4. Let peppers sit at room temperature for at least 3 days, though they will be better after 7 days. After 7 days, keep the peppers in the refrigerator.

Don't touch your eyes after cutting up these peppers or they'll burn.

COOKING SCHOOL

These hot banana pepper rings are made just like cucumber pickles. To make pickles, we soak vegetables in a mixture of vinegar, salt, and water (called **BRINE**) for a few days. The acid in the mixture gives the vegetables a sour taste.

SKINNY BERRY COOLATA

YIELD: 1 LARGE SHAKE

INGREDIENTS

- **2 cups** ice
- **1 cup** frozen strawberries (½ of a 16-oz bag), defrosted
- **¾–1 cup** any clear citrus-flavored diet soda (such as Sprite Zero or Fresca)
- **5** packets Splenda OR 2 Tbsp sugar

THOSE strawberry slushes at your local café are very refreshing, but who knows how much sugar and artificial stuff is packed into your plastic cup? This low-cal version has all the taste with none of the mystery. –V

INSTRUCTIONS

- In the jar of a blender, combine ice, strawberries, soda, and Splenda. Blend until fully combined.

> To make the strawberry coolatta in advance, freeze and then defrost in the refrigerator.

SNACK TIME

ICED VANILLA

YIELD 1 LARGE SHAKE

INGREDIENTS

- 2 cups ice
- 1 cup milk
- 2 Tbsp instant vanilla pudding powder
- 3 tsp pure vanilla extract
- 3 Tbsp sugar

A creamy coffee slush ... without the coffee! —L.

INSTRUCTIONS

- In the jar of a blender, combine ice, milk, pudding powder, vanilla, and sugar. Blend until fully combined.

> A little bit of pudding powder is the secret to creamy shakes. You'll need pure vanilla extract, though, for that real vanilla flavor. Imitation vanilla extract won't give you the same result.

HERE'S HOW!

MAKE OUR SWEET AND TART SOUR GUMMY RUGELACH (PAGE 108).

1 Roll your dough into a 10-inch circle.

2 Using a pizza slicer, cut the circle into 12 wedges.

3 Place a sour gummy bear on the wide side of each wedge.

4 Roll up one wedge at a time.

5 Dip the rugelach into egg white, and then into sugar. Place on a parchment-lined baking sheet.

DESSERTS

- TOFFEE-TOPPED BROWNIE CAKE — 96
- PEANUT BUTTER PIZZELLE CAKE — 98
- BANANA SUNDAE CAKE — 100
- CANDY BAR COOKIES — 102
- EGG-FREE SPRINKLE COOKIES — 104
- MEIRA'S POP 'EM COOKIES — 106
- SOUR GUMMY RUGELACH — 108
- CHOCOLATE PRETZEL BARS — 110
- STRAWBERRY SHORTCAKE — 112
- ICE CREAM RAZZLE — 114
- CHOCOLATE BONBONS — 116
- CONE CHIP COOKIE CUPS — 118
- CREAMSICLE SORBETS WITH CHOCOLATE WAFER POPS — 120
- RICE KRISPIES SANDWICHES — 122
- DESSERT STEP BY STEP — 124

TOFFEE-TOPPED BROWNIE CAKE

YIELD 24 BARS

INGREDIENTS

- 6 eggs
- 3 cups sugar
- 1½ cups oil
- 1½ cups flour
- 1½ cups cocoa
- 1½ tsp vanilla extract
- pinch salt
- 1½ cups orange juice
- 1½ tsp baking powder
- 2 (3.5 oz) good quality chocolate bars
- 6 Viennese Crunch (or chocolate-covered toffee bars)

EVERY good cook needs a basic brownie recipe … or one that's not so basic. This version is somewhere in the middle. It'll please the classic brownie lovers while making those who like something more special very happy. Thanks to Mrs. Saba Zolty for sharing this recipe!

—L.

INSTRUCTIONS

1. Preheat oven to 350°F. Line a baking sheet with parchment paper.

2. In the bowl of an electric mixer, combine eggs, sugar, and oil. Beat until mixture is creamy. Add in flour, cocoa, vanilla, salt, orange juice, and baking powder. Continue to beat until smooth.

3. Pour batter into prepared baking sheet. Use a spatula to spread the batter evenly.

4. Bake for 40-45 minutes. **TEST FOR DONENESS.**

5. Meanwhile, melt chocolate (see page 124). Spread melted chocolate over cake immediately after taking it out of the oven. Use a spatula to spread the chocolate evenly over the top.

6. Smash the Viennese Crunch into small bits. You can put them into a plastic bag and hit them with a mallet or the bottom of a heavy pan, or process them in a mini chopper. Sprinkle Viennese Crunch bits evenly over cake.

You must add the chocolate topping while the cake is still warm. The heat will help it spread evenly and easily.

We like Rosemarie, a praline-filled bittersweet chocolate bar.

COOKING SCHOOL

Use a toothpick to **TEST FOR DONENESS**. Carefully stick it into the center of the hot cake. The toothpick should come out clean, without any gooey batter attached. It's okay if there are some crumbs on the toothpick.

PEANUT BUTTER PIZZELLE CAKE

YIELD
1 CAKE; SERVES 16

INGREDIENTS

- **2 cups** confectioners' sugar
- **1 cup** peanut butter
- **4 cups** nondairy whipped topping OR heavy cream
- **1 Tbsp** pure vanilla extract
- **56-80** large pizzelle cookies

IN the past, a fridge was called an "icebox." That's why this is called an "icebox cake." You don't need an oven, but you do need to keep the cake in the fridge overnight before serving so that it's easy to slice.

–V.

INSTRUCTIONS

1 Prepare the peanut butter sugar: in the bowl of an electric mixer, combine confectioners' sugar and peanut butter. Mix on low speed until the mixture looks like peanut butter-flavored sugar. Remove from bowl and set aside.

2 Wipe the bowl. Pour whipped topping and vanilla into the bowl. Beat until STIFF PEAKS form.

3 Using an offset spatula, spread a little whipped topping on a large round cake plate so that the cookies stay in place. Arrange 6 cookies in a circle on the plate, with an additional cookie inside the circle. See step-by-step photos on page 126.

4 Spread a thin layer of cream on top of the cookies. This is easiest to do with an offset spatula, which has a long, flat metal head. If you don't have one, add the cream to a piping bag or resealable plastic bag with one corner snipped off, and pipe a swirl of cream over the cookies.

5 Sprinkle cream with about ¼ cup peanut butter sugar. Top with another layer of pizzelle cookies and continue to layer cookies, cream, and peanut butter sugar until the cake is 8-10 layers high. Refrigerate cake overnight before slicing.

To see how we make this cake step-by-step, see page 126.

See Resources, page 142, for where to find these pizzelles. You can use any thin store-bought cookies or your own cookies. Just make sure they are all the same size.

COOKING SCHOOL

How do you know when your whipped topping or whipped cream is ready? When you stop the mixer and lift up the whisk, the peaks that form will stand straight up and not move. This is called "STIFF PEAKS." The mixture will be thick. You can even turn the bowl upside down and your cream won't move. When the tips of the peaks fall back down, that's called "soft peaks." You'll need to beat the cream a bit more to reach the stiff peak stage.

BANANA SUNDAE CAKE

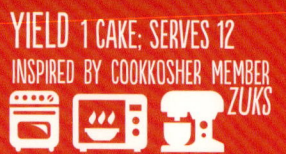

YIELD 1 CAKE; SERVES 12
INSPIRED BY COOKKOSHER MEMBER ZUKS

INGREDIENTS

- 3 eggs
- 2 cups sugar
- 1 cup oil
- 1 Tbsp baking soda
- 2 ripe bananas, peeled
- 1 cup water
- 2½ cups flour

MAGIC SHELL:
- 7 oz good quality baking chocolate
- 2 Tbsp oil

SUNDAE TOPPINGS:
- ½ cup chocolate chips
- ½ cup chopped peanuts
- ¼ cup toasted coconut or chocolate crunch

MAGIC shell is that hot chocolate that turns hard and crunchy when it's poured over ice cream. This cake also has a crunchy outside with a soft, moist cake inside. When you pour magic shell over the cake, it's automatically smooth. So you don't need to be a great cake decorator to get a perfect cake. –V.

INSTRUCTIONS

1. Preheat oven to 350°F. Grease and FLOUR a 3-quart stainless steel mixing bowl very well. You can use a floured baking spray instead.

2. In the bowl of an electric mixer, combine eggs and sugar. Beat on high speed until mixture is creamy. Slowly add in oil and continue to beat until combined.

3. With the mixer on low speed, add baking soda, bananas, water, and flour. Beat until combined. Pour batter into prepared mixing bowl. Bake until the center is no longer jiggly, 60-80 minutes. Let cake cool completely. Loosen cake edges with a knife, and invert onto a plate.

4. Prepare the magic shell: Melt chocolate (see page 124). Add oil and whisk until smooth.

5. Pour magic shell over cake and move the cake around so it's evenly coated with a thin layer of chocolate. Refrigerate cake for 5-7 minutes to set slightly, so the toppings don't run off the cake. Top with chocolate chips, peanuts, toasted coconut, or chocolate crunch. Refrigerate until chocolate is completely set. Serve at room temperature.

We used a stainless steel mixing bowl so the cake has a cool dome-like shape, but you can also use a Bundt pan.

COOKING SCHOOL

Sometimes, oil or nonstick cooking spray isn't enough to keep a cake from sticking to the pan. That's why we also like to **FLOUR** the baking pan. To flour your pan, first spray it very well with nonstick cooking spray. Then add a bit of flour to the pan and shake it until it's all covered with a thin layer of flour. Dump out any excess flour.

CANDY BAR COOKIES

YIELD 50 COOKIES

INGREDIENTS

- 1 cup (2 sticks) butter, melted
- 1 cup brown sugar
- ¾ cup sugar
- 2 eggs plus 1 egg yolk
- 1 tsp almond extract
- 2½ cups flour
- 1 cup cocoa
- 2 tsp baking powder
- ½ tsp salt
- ¾ cup chocolate chips
- 1 (2.64 oz) bag Kliks (or ¾ cup favorite chocolate candy)
- 1 cup chopped Milk Munch (or favorite chocolate bar)
- ½ cup chopped walnuts, toasted

HEAVEN.

No need to hide your favorite candy bars under your bed. You can now hide them in your cookie. You can still dream about them just as much.

-V.

INSTRUCTIONS

1. Preheat oven to 350°F. Line baking sheets with parchment paper (you will need 3 sheets to fit all the cookies, but you can bake them in batches).

2. In the bowl of an electric mixer, combine melted butter and SUGARS. Beat until creamy. Add in eggs and almond extract.

3. Slowly add in flour, cocoa, baking powder, and salt. Mix to combine.

4. Add chocolate chips, Kliks, Milk Munch, and walnuts. Mix to just combine.

5. Form batter into balls. Place about 2 inches apart on prepared baking sheets. Bake for 15 minutes. The cookies will still feel soft when they come out of the oven, but they will harden as they cool.

102 DESSERTS

Customize these cookies! Leah likes them with a Psek Zman candy bar and pecans instead of walnuts.

You can use a small ice cream scoop to help make your cookies evenly sized.

COOKING SCHOOL

BROWN SUGAR makes cookies moist, while **WHITE SUGAR** keeps them crispy. We usually use a combination of brown and white when we want a balanced cookie that's crispy-on-the-outside and moist-and-chewy-on-the-inside.

EGG-FREE SPRINKLE COOKIES

YIELD 24 COOKIES
INSPIRED BY COOKKOSHER MEMBER MWINER

INGREDIENTS

- **1 cup** (2 sticks) margarine or butter, at room temperature
- **¼ cup** sugar
- **⅔ cup** confectioners' sugar
- **1 tsp** vanilla extract
- **2 cups** flour
- **½ cup** rainbow sprinkles

So many kids are allergic to so many things nowadays, and eggs are one of the common allergies. I first made these for my niece Debbie so she wouldn't have to be left out when the other kids were enjoying cookies on Shabbat. When everyone wanted Debbie's cookies, I told her to take the cookie jar and hide it. Now, I make these cookies whether Debbie is around or not.

–V.

INSTRUCTIONS

1. Preheat oven to 375ºF. Line a baking sheet with parchment paper.

2. In the bowl of an electric MIXER fitted with a paddle attachment, beat margarine and sugars together until creamy. Add in vanilla and flour, and beat until a smooth dough forms. You will need to use a spatula to scrape down the sides of the bowl.

3. Roll dough into walnut-sized balls. Dip balls into rainbow sprinkles. Flatten them a bit as you dip them. Place on prepared baking sheet. They will not spread a lot, so you can place them close together and fit all the cookies on one baking sheet.

4. Bake for 15 minutes. Be careful not to overbake, as cookies will not turn very golden.

Don't be tempted to add baking powder to these cookies. Without the egg, the cookies will burn instead of rise.

COOKING SCHOOL

If you're using a stand **MIXER**, like a Kitchen Aid, there are three different attachments you can use for mixing: a dough hook, a paddle attachment, and a whisk attachment. The dough hook is best for making bread. The paddle attachment is best for mixing batter for cookies and cakes. The whisk attachment is used for whipping egg whites and cream. If you're using a bread mixer, like a Bosch, the dough hook is used for breads and dough, and the whisk attachment is used for most other batters.

MEIRA'S POP 'EM COOKIES

YIELD: 6-7 DOZEN MINI COOKIES

INGREDIENTS

- 1 cup quick cooking oats
- ⅔ cup whole wheat flour
- ½ cup sugar
- ½ tsp baking powder
- ½ tsp vanilla extract
- 2 eggs
- 6 Tbsp oil
- ¼ cup mini chocolate chips

KIDS have great recipe ideas too! We held a contest in AIM! Magazine (the tween magazine published by Ami) to find the one we loved the most. And the winner is … Meira Levy of Monsey, New York. Meira seems to be quite the cook already, as she sent in a whole bunch of her favorite recipes, including these fun cookies. When you start popping these, you'll never believe that they're healthier than your usual cookies.

—L

INSTRUCTIONS

1. Preheat oven to 350°F. Line two baking sheets with parchment paper.

2. In a large bowl, combine oats, flour, sugar, and BAKING POWDER. Add in vanilla, eggs, and oil. Using a wooden spoon, stir until completely combined.

   Fold in chocolate chips.

3. Using a ½-teaspoon measure, scoop out mini cookies and place on prepared baking sheets. They do not have to be far apart, as they will only spread a bit. Bake for 10 minutes. Let cool before you pop 'em.

106 DESSERTS

Whenever you're mixing a batter by hand, it's best if you combine all the dry ingredients, and then add the wet ingredients. This is not as important if you are using an electric mixer.

Of course, you can also make these into larger cookies, but that's not as much fun. Bake for a few minutes longer.

COOKING SCHOOL

When measuring **BAKING POWDER** or baking soda, level off the teaspoon. It's important to use the precise amount.

SOUR GUMMY RUGELACH

YIELD: 4 DOZEN RUGELACH

INGREDIENTS

- 2¼ cups flour, plus more for sprinkling
- 1 cup (2 sticks) margarine
- 1 cup nondairy whipped topping
- 1 egg yolk
- 1¼ tsp baking soda
- ¼ tsp salt
- 48 sour gummy bears
- 2 egg whites
- ½ cup sugar

MY sister-in-law can't forget the taste of Rina G.'s rugelach, even though she hasn't eaten them in 20 years. Why leave them as a memory? I phoned Rina and she dug up the old recipe. Rina used to hide a candy that's now extinct inside her rugelach, so I've replaced it with my favorite gummy bear. I also tried these rugelech with lots of other candies like jelly beans (not so great) and even sour belts (a little too sour for me, but some of the taste testers loved it!). —L.

INSTRUCTIONS

1. Preheat oven to 350°F. Line three baking sheets with parchment paper.

2. In the bowl of an electric mixer, combine flour, margarine, whipped topping, egg yolk, baking soda, and salt. Mix until dough is smooth. Divide into 4 balls.

3. Sprinkle flour on the top and bottom of each ball, so the dough doesn't stick. Working with one ball at a time, use a rolling pin to roll out a 10-inch circle. With a pizza slicer, cut dough into 12 triangles. See step-by-step photos on page 94.

4. Place a gummy bear on the wider end of each triangle. Place the edge of the dough over the gummy bear to cover it, and then ROLL UP the rugelah.

5. Place the egg whites into a bowl. Place the sugar into a second bowl. Dip each rugelah into the egg white, and then roll in the sugar. Place on prepared baking sheets. Bake for 10-12 minutes, or until golden. Let cool.

DESSERTS

For dairy rugelach, use butter instead of margarine, and heavy cream instead of nondairy whipped topping.

For a more elegant version, sprinkle sugar and chopped nuts onto the dough triangles before rolling. After baking, dust with confectioners' sugar.

See how we make rugelach step-by-step in "Here's How" on page 94.

COOKING SCHOOL

When we **ROLL UP** something "rugelach-style," we start at the wider end, so the thinnest point ends up on the outside, like on a croissant. When we want to roll a rectangular piece of dough into a cylinder, we roll it up "jelly roll-style."

CHOCOLATE PRETZEL BARS

YIELD 20 BARS

INGREDIENTS

4 oz	salted pretzels, crushed (about 1¼ cup crumbs)
¼ cup	brown sugar
⅔ cup	oil
1	egg white
8 oz	bittersweet baking chocolate, finely chopped
1 cup	nondairy whipped topping

CHOCOLATE-COVERED PRETZELS:

2 oz	bittersweet baking chocolate
30	mini salted pretzels

LOVE chocolate-covered pretzels? There's something about salty and sweet together that's irresistible. And that combination is even better in these bars. Make sure to choose a pretzel brand that you love and add the salt from the bottom of the bag into your crust.

—V.

INSTRUCTIONS

1. Preheat oven to 350°F. Grease an 8 x 8-inch baking pan or LINE with parchment paper.

2. In the bowl of a food processor, process pretzels, brown sugar, oil, and egg white until combined.

3. Add mixture to pan, pressing down with a spoon to smooth it. Bake for 12 minutes.

4. Place chocolate into a bowl. In a small saucepan, bring whipped topping to a boil over high heat. Pour over chocolate. Let sit for 3-4 minutes, as the hot whipped topping helps to melt the chocolate.

See step-by-step photos on page 125.

5. Whisk chocolate mixture until smooth (if there are any lumps left, microwave for 15 seconds and whisk again). Pour over crust. Place in refrigerator or freezer until firm.

6. Prepare the chocolate-covered pretzels: Melt chocolate (see page 124). Dip half of each pretzel into chocolate. Place them onto wax or parchment paper to set.

7. When chocolate layer is firm, top with chocolate-covered pretzels. Keep frozen; cut into bars to serve.

Someone will likely want to munch on your chocolate-covered pretzels so it's a good idea to make some extra.

The chocolate topping to these pretzel bars is called "chocolate ganache." See how we make it step-by-step on page 125.

COOKING SCHOOL

LINE your baking pan with parchment paper to make it easier to remove the entire cake at once. To avoid crinkly corners, cut two 8-inch wide pieces of parchment paper. Place them into the baking pan in opposite directions.

STRAWBERRY SHORTCAKE

YIELD 8 SERVINGS

INGREDIENTS

VANILLA STREUSEL:
- ½ cup flour
- 1 pkg (3.5 oz) vanilla pudding powder (not sugar-free)
- 1 tsp vanilla extract
- ¼ cup oil

STRAWBERRY STREUSEL:
- ½ cup flour
- 1 pkg (3-oz) strawberry jell dessert powder (we used Kolatin brand)
- 1 tsp vanilla extract
- ¼ cup oil

ICE CREAM:
- 8 oz frozen strawberries, defrosted
- 1 quart vanilla ice cream, slightly thawed

WHEN *I was a kid, my favorite treat from the ice cream truck was an ice cream bar coated with strawberry and vanilla crumbs. Now, I can make that treat in my own kitchen (and there's enough for everyone).* —V.

INSTRUCTIONS

1. Preheat oven to 350°F. Line a baking sheet with parchment paper or grease with nonstick cooking spray.

2. Prepare the vanilla STREUSEL: In a small bowl, combine flour, vanilla pudding powder, vanilla, and oil. Using a spoon, stir until ingredients are combined and the mixture looks like crumbs.

3. Prepare the strawberry streusel: In a small bowl, combine flour, strawberry jell dessert powder, vanilla, and oil. Using a spoon, stir until ingredients are combined and the mixture looks like crumbs.

4. Place all the streusel crumbs side by side on prepared baking sheet. Bake for 15 minutes. Let cool.

5. Prepare the ice cream: In the bowl of a food processor, purée strawberries with their juice until completely liquefied.

6. In a large bowl, combine softened vanilla ice cream and strawberry purée. Using a spoon, swirl strawberry purée into ice cream. (You can also use an electric mixer to make this step easier—but don't mix too much or you won't have those swirls.) Pour into a springform pan. Freeze for 15-20 minutes.

7. Once ice cream is slightly set, top with crumbs. Keep frozen until ready to serve.

112 DESSERTS

If you want to make a pareve strawberry ice cream from scratch to go with these crumbs, whip 1 cup nondairy whipped topping. Add in ¾ cup sugar, 3 egg yolks, and 1 cup strawberry purée. Freeze until firm.

We used a mini springform pan to make the strawberry shorcake in the photo, but you can make this dessert in any bowl, baking pan, glass dish, or mini ramekins.

COOKING SCHOOL

STREUSEL is a crumb topping that usually goes on top of cakes and muffins ... and now ice cream! When you make your streusel, make sure it looks like crumbs of all different sizes. Don't try to mix it until it's smooth.

ICE CREAM RAZZLE

YIELD 2 SMALL RAZZLES

INGREDIENTS

- **4 scoops** vanilla ice cream
- **1 Tbsp** milk
- **2 Tbsp** caramel sauce, plus more for the top
- **½ cup** Rice Krispies, plus more for the top
- **2 Tbsp** chocolate chips, plus more for the top
- **3** chocolate sandwich cookies, crushed

WANT to make a dairy ice cream razzle without investing in a razzle machine? The trick to a good razzle is not to blend too much, or you'll end up with ice cream mush (which is good, but not as good as when ice cream has crunchy bits in it).

—L.

INSTRUCTIONS

1. Place vanilla ice cream into a food processor and let it defrost slightly, 5-10 minutes.

2. Blend ice cream for 5 seconds. Add milk, caramel sauce, Rice Krispies, chocolate chips, and crushed sandwich cookies. Blend for 2 seconds. Pour into 2 large cups. Freeze for 5-10 minutes.

3. Top razzle with more Rice Krispies and chocolate chips. Drizzle with more caramel sauce. Eat right away.

What else can you add to a razzle? We also like rainbow sprinkles and peanut crunch.

COOKING SCHOOL

As you become an experienced cook, you'll quickly learn when a recipe needs to be followed precisely and when you can customize it as you like. An ice cream razzle is one of those times when you can make a recipe your own. For a double chocolate razzle, swap the caramel for chocolate syrup. For a peanut butter razzle, swap the caramel for peanut butter and add nut crunch. For a cappuccino razzle, replace the milk with (decaf!) coffee.

CHOCOLATE BONBONS

YIELD 24 BONBONS

INGREDIENTS

- 24   chocolate sandwich cookies
- 1 pint   favorite flavor ice cream
- 10 oz   good quality bittersweet chocolate, *finely chopped*
- ¼ cup   toasted coconut

THIS is the sweet treat that both the kids and adults in my family request most often. I really can't complain when they want it every week since it's so simple to make.

—V.

INSTRUCTIONS

1. Place chocolate sandwich cookies onto a baking sheet.

2. Using a melon baller and working quickly, place a small scoop of ice cream on the center of each cookie. Place baking sheet in the freezer. See step-by-step photos on pages 128-129.

3. Melt CHOCOLATE (see page 124).

4. Remove bonbon tray from the freezer. Hold each bonbon over the melted chocolate and spoon the chocolate over the bonbon to cover. Return bonbon to the baking sheet and sprinkle with coconut. The chocolate hardens quickly, so the topping needs to be sprinkled on immediately or it won't stick. Repeat with remaining bonbons.

5. Return to freezer until ready to serve.

DESSERTS

If your bonbons are melting too quickly in step 4, you can take just half of them out of the freezer at a time. Take the other half out of the freezer when the first batch is done.

Any ice cream topping will work.

See how we do it on pages 128-129.

COOKING SCHOOL

How do you know if **CHOCOLATE** is "good quality"? Good quality bittersweet or semisweet chocolate bars sometimes have the percentage of cacao printed on the package; it should be 55 percent cacao or above. Some reliable pareve chocolate brands include Alprose, Schmerling, Torino, and Scharffen Berger.

CONE CHIP COOKIE CUPS

YIELD 10 CUPS

INGREDIENTS

- ½ cup oil
- ½ cup sugar
- ½ cup brown sugar
- 1 egg
- 1 tsp vanilla extract
- ½ tsp baking powder
- pinch salt
- 1¼ cups flour
- 1 cup crushed sugar cones (about 6 cones)
- ½ cup chocolate chips
- 1 quart vanilla ice cream

IF a chocolate chip cookie is going to be served with ice cream, it makes sense that it should include bits of cone inside. It also makes sense that the cookie should be in the shape of a cup, so it can hold the ice cream.
-L.

INSTRUCTIONS

1. Preheat oven to 350°F. Line a 12-cup muffin pan with paper liners.

2. In the bowl of an electric mixer, beat oil, sugars, and eggs until creamy. Add in vanilla, baking powder, salt, and flour and beat until combined. With mixer on low speed, add in crushed sugar cones and chocolate chips.

3. Using an ice cream scoop, place a scoop of dough into each muffin cup and press down the center to form a cup shape. Bake for 18-20 minutes. Let cool completely before removing from muffin pan.

4. When ready to serve, top cookie cups with a scoop of ICE CREAM.

DESSERTS

If you're serving these for dessert and you won't have time to scoop ice cream onto each cup, you can scoop the ice cream in advance and keep the ice cream balls in the freezer so they're ready to go.

COOKING SCHOOL

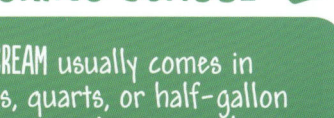

ICE CREAM usually comes in pints, quarts, or half-gallon containers. A quart is the same as two pints, or half of a half-gallon. See "Beyond Measure" on page 6.

CREAMSICLE SORBETS with CHOCOLATE WAFER POPS

YIELD 8 SERVINGS

INGREDIENTS

- **2 cups** nondairy whipped topping, divided
- **1 pint** mango sorbet, partially defrosted
- **1 pint** coconut sorbet, partially defrosted

CHOCOLATE WAFER POPS:
- **16** chocolate wafer rolls
- **4 oz** chocolate
- **16** skewers

READY

to make an elegant dessert for your family? Being a good cook isn't only about knowing how to cook and bake, it's also knowing how you can "fake it" and let everyone think that you've made something amazing from scratch.

—L.

INSTRUCTIONS

1. To the bowl of an electric mixer, add 1 cup nondairy whipped topping. For a creamier, light creamsicle, whip the nondairy topping until stiff. For a thicker creamsicle that is easier to scoop, you can skip this step.

2. Add the mango sorbet to the whipped topping. Beat until combined. Pour sorbet into a container. Use a SCRAPING SPATULA to get all the sorbet. Freeze. Repeat with remaining 1 cup nondairy whipped topping and coconut sorbet.

3. Prepare the chocolate wafer pops: Carefully push a skewer through the center of each wafer roll.

4. Melt chocolate (see page 124). Carefully dip each wafer stick into the melted chocolate. Place on a piece of parchment or wax paper. To avoid a flat side, insert the stick into an apple or piece of Styrofoam until chocolate is set. See step-by-step photos on page 127.

5. To serve, scoop sorbet into individual dishes and serve with two wafer rolls.

120 DESSERTS

You can use any good-quality sorbet flavor for the creamsicles, such as passion fruit or strawberry.

For an easier presentation, you can layer the two creamsicle flavors in a glass trifle bowl. Make sure the first layer is completely frozen before adding the second.

See how we make these chocolate wafer pops on page 127.

COOKING SCHOOL

When getting every last bit of sorbet or cake batter out of your bowl, you'll use a **SCRAPING SPATULA**. They usually are made of rubber or silicone. For more on different types of spatulas, see Cooking School on pages 29 and 123.

RICE KRISPIES SANDWICHES

YIELD 24 SQUARES

INGREDIENTS

- ¼ cup (½ stick) margarine or butter
- 1 (16-oz) container marshmallow fluff
- 8 cups Rice Krispies
- 1 quart ice cream, slightly defrosted
- ¾ cup sprinkles or chocolate chips

I always knew I loved Rice Krispies Treats, but now I love them way more with ice cream in the middle. I'll never make plain Rice Krispies Treats again. —V.

INSTRUCTIONS

1. Melt margarine in a medium saucepan over medium heat. Add fluff and mix until margarine and fluff are completely combined. Stir in Rice Krispies, 1 cup at a time.

2. Divide the Rice Krispies Treats mixture between two 9 x 13-inch baking pans and press into a thin layer.

3. Top one Rice Krispies layer with softened ice cream. Spread ice cream into an even layer using an OFFSET SPATULA. Top with sprinkles or chocolate chips. Freeze ice cream layer for 30 minutes to 1 hour, until ice cream is firm.

4. Place second Rice Krispies layer over firm ice cream. Using a sharp knife, cut into squares. This is easier to do when the top layer is not yet frozen. Return to freezer until ready to serve.

DESSERTS

This is easier to do if you drop some Rice Krispies Treats all over the bottom of the pan rather than in one spot. You can also place a piece of wax paper over them as you press down to help you flatten them evenly.

COOKING SCHOOL

Flattening your ice cream will be easiest if you use an **OFFSET SPATULA**. It's also the best type of spatula to use when icing a cake, like we did in the Peanut Butter Pizzelle Cake (see how we smooth out the icing on page 126). For more on spatulas, see Cooking School on pages 29 and 121.

DESSERT STEP BY STEP

MELTING CHOCOLATE IN THE MICROWAVE

THE traditional way to melt chocolate is using a double boiler. A double boiler is a pot or bowl placed over a pot of simmering water. Melting chocolate in the microwave is much quicker and neater.

Use the following method of melting chocolate when making Toffee-Topped Brownie Cake (page 96), Banana Sundae Cake (page 100), Chocolate-Covered Pretzels (page 110), Chocolate Bonbons (page 116), and Chocolate Wafer Pops (page 120).

1. Chop up your chocolate and place it into a microwave-safe bowl.

2. Microwave the chocolate for 1 minute. Remove from microwave and stir.

3. Microwave for an additional 30 seconds. The chocolate might still look lumpy when you take it out of the microwave, but should become smooth as you stir. Your chocolate is ready to use.

4. If there are still lumps in your chocolate, microwave for 15 more seconds.

MAKING CHOCOLATE GANACHE

WE used chocolate ganache as the top layer in our Chocolate Pretzel Bars (page 110). You can also use chocolate ganache to ice a cake or frost a cupcake. Let it cool first to room temperature and it will thicken to the consistency of frosting.

When chocolate ganache is hot, you can use it as a chocolate sauce on top of ice cream. When chocolate ganache is cold, it will become firm and turn into chocolate fudge.

1. Chop 8 oz chocolate and place it into a glass bowl. (Plastic will not work as well because it doesn't retain heat.)

2. Heat 1 cup nondairy whipped topping or heavy cream in a small saucepan. As soon as it comes to a boil, pour it over the chocolate.

3. Let the mixture sit for 3-4 minutes as the hot liquid melts the chocolate.

4. Stir carefully until smooth.

5. If there are any lumps of chocolate left after you've stirred for awhile, microwave ganache for 15 seconds and stir again.

PEANUT BUTTER PIZZELLE CAKE

SURPRISE *a birthday boy or girl with this impressive but easy-to-make cake.*

Page 98

1. Using an offset spatula, spread some whipped topping on a large cake stand to prevent the cookies from moving.

2. You will need seven cookies for each cake layer. Place 6 cookies in a circle on the cake stand. Place 1 cookie in the center.

3. Spread a thin layer of whipped topping over the cookies. You can use an offset spatula to spread the whipped topping, as we did in step 1, or you can place the whipped topping into a piping bag or resealable plastic bag (with the corner snipped

126 DESSERTS

off) and pipe a spiral onto the cookies. (The whipped topping will spread when you place the next layer of cookies on top, so don't worry if the cookies are not fully covered.)

4 Sprinkle peanut butter sugar on top of whipped topping.

5 Top with another layer of cookies. For a prettier cake, place each cookie in between the cookies in the previous layer, rather than directly over them.

6 Repeat until you have 8 to 10 layers. Place cake in the refrigerator overnight before serving (it will soften and be easy to slice).

To make a peanut butter drizzle for the top of the cake, as seen on the photo on page 99, microwave some peanut butter for 20 seconds. Stir, then microwave again for 20 seconds. Stir again. Fill a piping bag with the peanut butter and drizzle lines over the cake.

CHOCOLATE WAFER POPS
Page 120

WE served these Chocolate Wafer Pops with our Creamsicle Sorbet. You can make perfect wafer pops too and serve them with any dessert to add an elegant touch. Here's how we do it.

1 Carefully insert a skewer into each chocolate wafer roll.

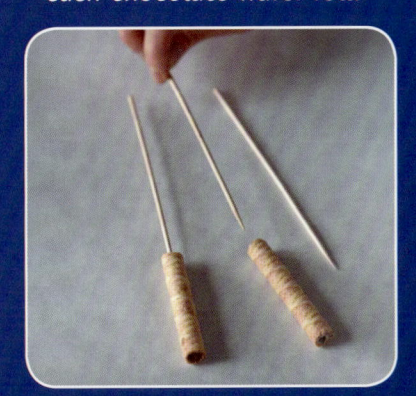

Continues on the next page.

Continued from the previous page.

2. Melt chocolate (see page 124). Spoon chocolate over wafer roll, coating evenly, or, for easy dipping, place the chocolate in a tall, narrow cup to coat evenly.

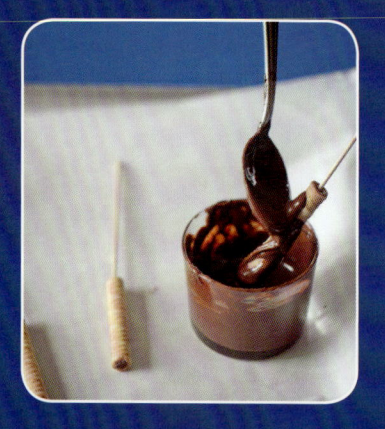

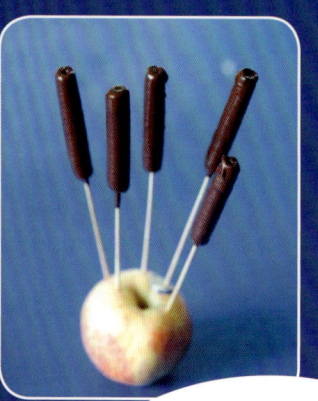

3. Stick the skewers into an apple or a piece of Styrofoam to dry. You can leave the apple and wafer pops on the counter, or place into the refrigerator for quicker drying. Once dry, remove the wafer pops from the apple. Keep in freezer until ready to use.

> Don't let this apple go to waste! After your wafer pops have dried, slice the apple and dip the slices into the leftover chocolate for a treat.

CHOCOLATE BONBONS
Page 116

1. Place the chocolate sandwich cookies on a baking sheet.

2. Using a melon baller or small ice cream scoop, scoop balls of ice cream or sorbet and place one on each cookie. Place the baking sheet into the freezer while you melt the chocolate.

3. Melt the chocolate (see page 124). Remove baking sheet from freezer (you might want to remove only half the bonbons at a time, so the ice cream balls don't melt while you are working). Carefully spoon chocolate over the ice cream and the edges of the cookie. Let extra chocolate drip back into the bowl.

4. Place bonbon on the baking sheet and immediately sprinkle with toasted coconut or desired topping. The chocolate dries quickly, so work fast! Return to freezer. Keep frozen until ready to serve.

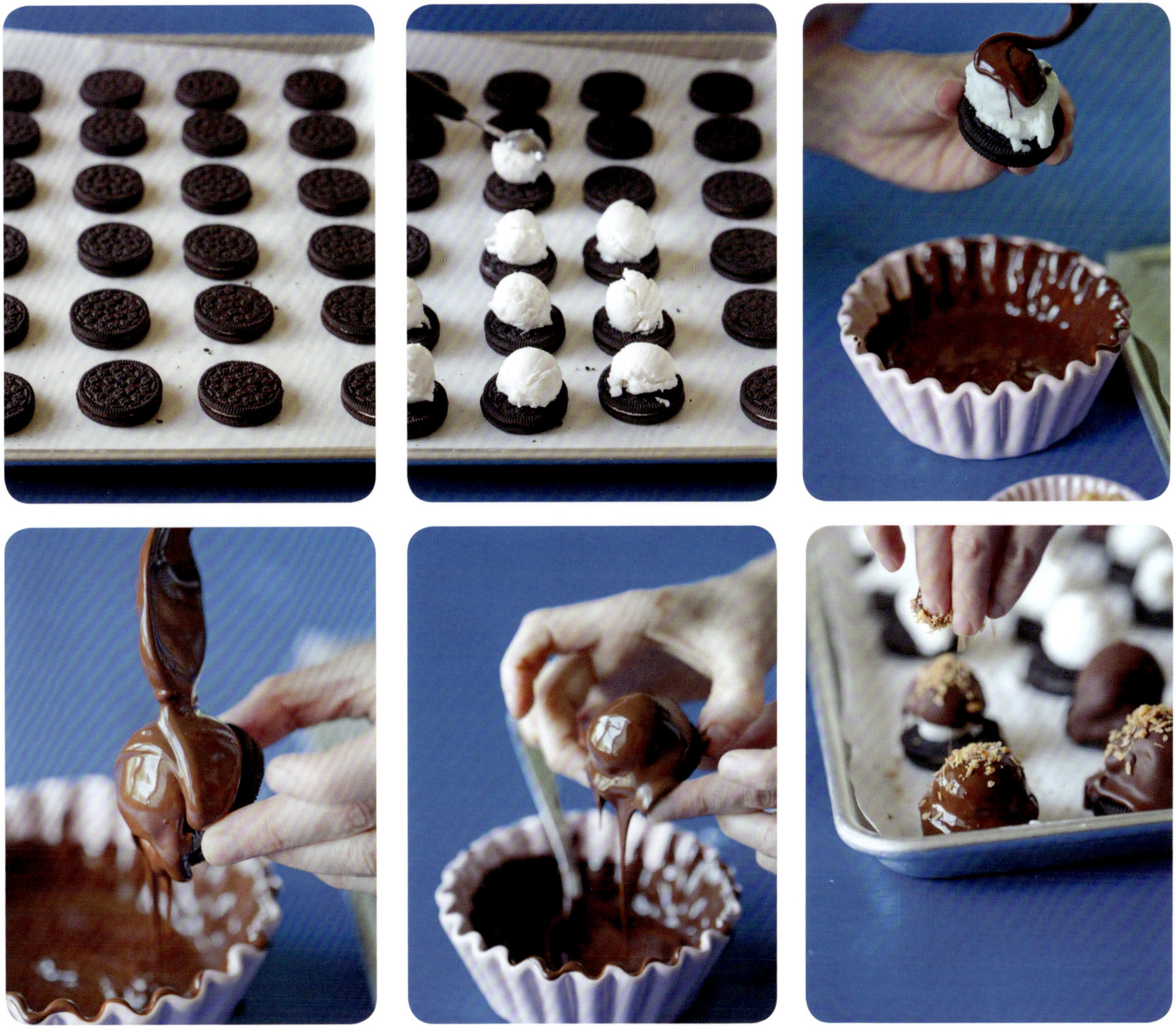

HERE'S HOW!

LEARN THE NO-MESS WAY TO FILL A PIPING BAG WITH ICING TO CREATE BUTTON CANDY (PAGE 132).

1 Place some icing in the center of a piece of plastic wrap.

2 Fold over the two sides.

3 Twist the two ends very tightly.

4 Drop the wrapped icing into a piping bag, pushing one end of the plastic through the tip.

5 Snip off the extra plastic. When the icing is used up, simply pull out the plastic wrap and throw it away. Your clean piping bag can be used again.

BUTTON CANDY 132	EDIBLE SAND ART 136	CANDY MANCALA 140
CANDY SPRAY 134	MICRO-DOUGH 138	ZOUR PEG SOLITAIRE 140
		MARSHMALLOW ERECTOR SET 141

SWEETS AND CRAFTS

BUTTON CANDY

YIELD 50-60 STRIPS

INGREDIENTS

- **1** (1-lb) box confectioners' sugar (about 4 cups)
- **3 Tbsp** meringue powder
- **⅓ cup** water, plus more for thinning icing
- food coloring, (see "Cooking School" on page 137)
- flavored extracts

EQUIPMENT:
- copy paper, cut into 3 long strips

WHENEVER I buy button candy for my children for a Shabbat treat, I make them share with me. Now that we can make them at home, we don't have to fight over our favorite flavors. Besides unlimited buttons, the best part of making your own is the ability to match the buttons to the color scheme of a party.

–V.

INSTRUCTIONS

1. In the bowl of an electric mixer fitted with the paddle attachment, combine confectioners' sugar and meringue powder. Mix on low speed to combine.

2. Add water and mix on low speed until combined. Raise speed to high and beat until stiff peaks form, 5 minutes.

3. Divide **ROYAL ICING** into bowls, one bowl for each flavor. Add ½ teaspoon water at a time to each bowl, mixing thoroughly, until the icing is the consistency of toothpaste. Add a few drops of food coloring and ½ teaspoon flavored extract (see button candy flavors on the next page) and mix to combine. Cover bowls until ready for the next step. **See step-by-step photos on page 130.**

4. Add each icing color to a different piping bag fitted with a round tip. Pipe little dots in rows on the strips of copy paper. Let dry overnight.

SWEETS & CRAFTS

Learn our no-mess method for filling piping bags with icing in "Here's How" on page 130.

For perfectly lined-up dots, mark your dots with a pen on a piece of graph paper. Place your copy paper strips over your graph paper template.

If you can't find meringue powder at your supermarket or grocery, you can get it at kitchen supply shops.

BUTTON CANDY FLAVORS

Red/Pink Color	Orange Color	Yellow or Green Color	Blue Color	White Color	
Strawberry Extract	Orange Extract	Lemon Extract	Raspberry Extract	Coconut Extract	Use vanilla extract if you are missing extract for any color.

COOKING SCHOOL

The icing used for this button candy is called **ROYAL ICING**. It's the same type that is used to ice sugar cookies. It dries hard when exposed to air, so keep your icing covered at all times when not using it. For easy storage, mix your icing in plastic containers that come with a tight-fitting lid.

CANDY SPRAY

YIELD 4 SPRAY BOTTLES

INGREDIENTS

- ½ cup sugar
- ½ cup plus 2 Tbsp water, divided
- ½ tsp raspberry or strawberry extract (optional)
- 1 Tbsp citric acid (also called sour salt)

EQUIPMENT:
- 4 3-ounce spray bottles

I meant to ask the dentist if candy spray is a better alternative to sticky taffies when a kid wants a treat. After all, there's no chewing involved. This one isn't yet dentist-approved, but it's still fun to make on your own.

—L.

INSTRUCTIONS

1. In a small saucepan over medium-high heat, combine sugar, ½ cup water, and optional extract. Bring to a boil and stir until dissolved, about 1 minute.

2. Stir in CITRIC ACID and remaining 2 tablespoons water.

3. Fill spray bottles and let cool before spritzing.

Candy spray is delicious on its own, so you don't need to run to the store to buy flavors. If you're trying new flavors, the raspberry and strawberry versions are delicious, but beware — don't try cherry! Cherry extract tastes like medicine.

COOKING SCHOOL

CITRIC ACID naturally comes from lemons and limes. It's what gives sour sticks and other candy their sour flavor. Citric acid looks like a white powder and is also called sour salt. We use it to give tanginess to our Candy Spray and Edible Sand Art on page 136. You can find it in the spice section of the supermarket.

EDIBLE SAND ART

YIELD ½ CUP

INGREDIENTS

FOR EACH COLOR:

- ½ **cup** sugar
- ¾ **tsp** citric acid (also called sour salt)
- 3 drops food coloring
- winkie pops (optional)

EQUIPMENT:

- small plastic or glass jars

"**I'M** so booooorrrrred." The three words no mother wants to hear. Well, you shouldn't be bored anymore once you have this book. Read, color, bake, or make sand art!

—L.

INSTRUCTIONS

1. In a resealable plastic bag, combine sugar, citric acid, and FOOD COLORING. Seal the bag. Shake until all the sugar is colored. Repeat, using a new bag for each color, making as many different colors as you like.

2. Spoon sugar through a funnel into a glass or plastic container, alternating colors.

3. Optional: Dip your winkie pop into the sugar to enjoy.

You can use simple bottles from your drugstore for your sand art, like we did. If you're having a party, though, and want to make this a great activity, you can find sand art bottles in different shapes online at low prices. You'll also need a funnel. Choose bottles with wide necks if you want to dip your winkie pop, or place sand into bowls for dipping.

COOKING SCHOOL

Don't have so many different bottles of FOOD COLORING? No problem. Mix and match to make new shades. Purple = 1 drop blue + 3 drops red; Orange = 1 drop red + 2 drops yellow; Lime Green = 3 drops yellow + 1 drop green; Aqua = 2 drops blue + 1 drop green.

MICRO-DOUGH

YIELD 1 POUND DOUGH

INGREDIENTS

- *1 cup* flour
- *½ cup* salt
- *1 tsp* cream of tartar
- *1 cup* warm water
- *2 Tbsp* oil
- food coloring, (see "Cooking School" on page 137)

RAINING outside? You have all the ingredients you need to make play-dough right in your pantry. It's easiest and quickest to make play-dough in the microwave. Make lots of colors. Mom won't mind because there'll be no dirty pots. **Note: This dough should not be eaten; it's meant for play only.** —V.

INSTRUCTIONS

1. Place flour, salt, and cream of tartar into a medium MICROWAVE-SAFE bowl. Stir to combine.

2. Add water, oil, and food coloring to a measuring cup. Whisk to blend food coloring.

3. Slowly pour wet ingredients into dry ingredients, stirring until there are no lumps. Microwave for 2 minutes.

4. Remove from microwave. You will see the mixture at the edges and bottom of the bowl will already look like play-dough. Using a wooden spoon, push the cooked dough down and mix it back into the rest of the mixture.

5. Microwave for 1 more minute. The mixture should now look like dough and not be runny. If it is still a bit sticky, microwave for 30 more seconds, or until dough is no longer sticky. Let cool before handling.

The food coloring that is available in the supermarket will give you pale dough. For bold colors, you can find higher quality gel food coloring at kitchen supply and craft stores.

Cream of tartar is what gives the play-dough its flexibility. It's available in the spice section of your supermarket.

COOKING SCHOOL

Not all dishes are MICROWAVE-SAFE. Glass, ceramic, paper, and some plastics can be microwaved, but never, ever put metal or aluminum in the microwave — or sparks will fly.

GAMES TO PLAY...
AND EAT WHEN YOU'RE DONE

CANDY MANCALA

EACH PLAYER places 4 gumballs or candies in each cup on his or her side of a clean egg carton. Each player will also need an extra bowl on each side of the carton for his or her "store." When it's your turn, pick up all the candies in one of your cups. Moving counterclockwise, drop one candy into each cup until you have no more. If you pass your store, drop in one candy, but don't drop one in your opponent's store. If the last piece that you drop is in an empty cup on your side, take that candy and all your opponent's candy from the cup on the opposite side and keep it in your store. The game ends when one side is empty. The player with the most candy wins.

ZOUR PEG SOLITAIRE

PREHEAT OVEN to 350ºF. Grease an 8-inch round aluminum pan. Use a ½ recipe of our Egg-Free Sprinkle Cookies on page 104 to make one giant cookie. Place cookie in the prepared pan and flatten. Using a straw, make 3 rows of 9 holes each in both directions (see photo). Bake for 18-20 minutes. When the cookie comes out of the oven, use the straw again to widen the holes.

To play, fill all the holes except the center hole with Zours or Mike and Ikes. Play by jumping one candy over another into an empty hole. When a candy peg is hopped over, remove it from the game board. The goal of the game is to remove all candy from the board except for one, and it should end up in the center hole.

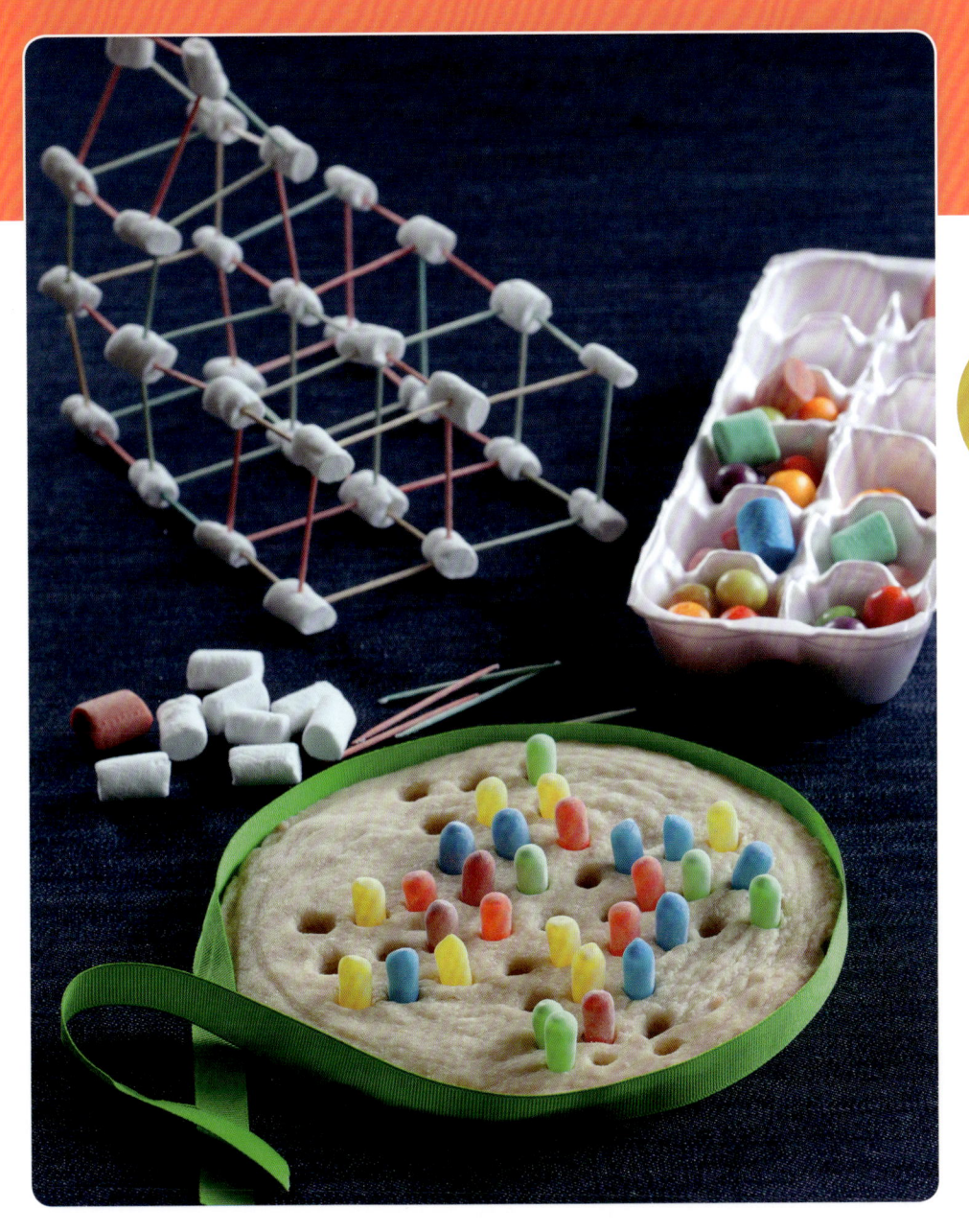

MARSHMALLOW ERECTOR SET

FILL PLASTIC cups with water and add a few drops of food coloring to each. Add toothpicks to the water and let them soak for 5 minutes. Remove from water and let dry. Use the colored toothpicks to connect mini marshmallows and start building.

SOURCES

MASON JARS. Available in supermarkets, hardware stores, kitchen supply, stores, and big box stores. Shown on pages 10, 53, 69, and 91.

SPORKS. Available at party supply stores where disposable bamboo dishes are sold. Shown on page 19.

STRIPED PAPER STRAWS. Available at kitchen supply stores or online at shopsweetlulu.com. Shown on pages 10, 43, 53, 57, 92, 93, 103

MYDRAP CLOTH NAPKINS AND PLACEMATS. Available in rolls of 12 in 7 sizes and over 30 colors and styles at www.buymydrap.com. Shown on pages 17, 21, 29, 43, and 75.

COLORFUL CHOPSTICKS. Available at CB2.com. Shown on page 49.

PIZZELLE COOKIES. The cookies we used are made by Reko brand. We found them at Costco and BJs. Other retailers include ShopRite, Stop and Shop, and Pathmark stores. See pizzellecookies.com for more retailers.

SPRAY BOTTLES. Available at Target. Shown on pages 135 and 137.

K-I-D-S LETTERS. Available at Target. Shown on pages 123 and 135.

FIRST TIME IN THE KITCHEN?

Start with these recipes with relatively little help.

Pancake "Sandwiches," *page 32*

Ramen Deli Salad, *page 48*

Peach and Mango Salad, *page 66*

Sugar Snap Peas and Edamame, *page 70*

Onion n' Garlic Popcorn, *page 80*

Grab and Go Muffins, *page 86*

Meira's Pop 'Ems, *page 106*

Edible Sand Art, *page 136*

Micro-Dough, *page 138*

INDEX

A
ALMONDS
  Ramen Deli Salad, *48*
AVOCADOS
  Panini Wraps, *24*
  slicing, *25*
  Taco Night, *44*

B
Banana Sundae Cake, *100*
Barbecue Sauce, DIY, *40*
BEEF
  Hot Dog Garlic Knots, *52*
  Malafel, *56*
  Meat and Potato Knishes, *54–55*
  Sino Steak Sandwiches, *46–47*
  Sticks, Teriyaki, *50*
  Taco Night, *44*
Bon Bons, chocolate, *116, 128*
Borekas, Broccoli-Cheese, *30*
Bow-Tie Chips, Toasted, *82*
BREADS
  Cheesy Pita Chips, *21*
  Grab and Go Muffins, *86*
  Hot Pretzels, *78*
Broccoli-Cheese Borekas, *30*
Brownie Cake, Toffee-Topped, *96*
Button Candy, *132*

C
CABBAGE
  Malafel, *56*
  Purple Salad, *57*

CAKES
  Banana Sundae, *100*
  Peanut Butter Pizzelle, *98*
  Toffee-Topped Brownie, *96*
Candy Bar Cookies, *102*
Candy, Button, *132*
Candy Mancala, *140*
Candy Spray, *134*
Cauliflower Poppers, *72*
CHEESE
  -Broccoli Borekas, *30*
  Deep Dish Personal Pizza, *22*
  Panini Wraps, *24*
  Pita Packets, *26*
  Pizza Soup, *20*
  Spinach Quesadillas, *28*
Chewy PB Granola Bars, *88*
CHICKEN
  with DIY Barbecue Sauce, *40*
  Nuggets, Honey BBQ, *36*
  over French Fries, *42*
  Sticks, Grilled, *38*
CHOCOLATE
  Banana Sundae Cake, *100*
  Bonbons, *116, 128*
  Candy Bar Cookies, *102*
  Chewy PB Granola Bars, *88*
  Cone Chip Cookie Cups, *118*
  ganache, preparing, *125*
  Grab and Go Muffins, *86*
  Ice Cream Razzle, *114*
  Meira's Pop'em Cookies, *106*
  melting in the microwave, *124*
  Pretzel Bars, *110*
  Toffee-Topped Brownie Cake, *96*
  Wafer Pops, Creamsicle Sorbets with, *120, 127-128*

COCONUT
  Banana Sundae Cake, *100*
  Chocolate Bonbons, *116*
Cone Chip Cookie Cups, *118*
Cookie Cups, Cone Chip, *118*
COOKIES AND BARS
  Candy Bar Cookies, *102*
  Chewy PB Granola Bars, *88*
  Chocolate Pretzel Bars, *110*
  Cone Chip Cookie Cups, *118*
  Egg-Free Sprinkle Cookies, *104*
  Meira's Pop'em Cookies, *106*
  Sour Gummy Rugelach, *108*
COOKING BASICS
  before and after cooking, *11*
  conversions, *6*
  garlic, *9*
  guide to the recipes, *12–13*
  making half a recipe, *11*
  measuring, *6–7*
  onions, *8*
  setting the table, *10*
Creamsicle Sorbets with Chocolate Wafer Pops, *120, 127-128*
Creamy Orzo, *18*

D
Deep Dish Personal Pizza, *22*
DELI
  Hot Dog Garlic Knots, *52*
  Meat and Potato Knishes, *54–55*
  Ramen Deli Salad, *48*
DIPS AND SAUCES
  DIY Barbecue Sauce, *40*
  Honey-Garlic Sauce, *42*
  Honey Mustard Dip, *72*
  Panini Dip, *24*
  Red Pepper Dip, *68*
  Salsa, *84*
  Strawberry Sauce, *32*
  Tartar Sauce, *59*
DRINKS
  Iced Vanilla, *93*
  Skinny Berry Coolata, *92*

E
Edamame and Sugar Snap Peas, *70*
Edible Sand Art, *136*
Egg-Free Sprinkle Cookies, *104*
Everything Fish Sticks, *58*

F
Fish Sticks, Everything, *58*

G
GAMES
  Candy Mancala, *140*
  Marshmallow Erector Set, *140*
  Zour Peg Solitaire, *140*
Garlic, *9*
Garlic Popcorn, Onion n', *80*
Grab and Go Muffins, *86*
Granola Bars, Chewy PB, *88*
Grilled Chicken Sticks, *38*

H
Honey BBQ Chicken Nuggets, *36*
Honey-Garlic Sauce, *42*
Honey Mustard Dip, *72*
Hot Banana Peppers, *90*
Hot Dog Garlic Knots, *52*
Hot Pretzels, *78*

I
ICE CREAM
  Chocolate Bonbons, *116*
  Cone Chip Cookie Cups, *118*
  Razzle, *114*
  Rice Krispies Sandwiches, *122*

Strawberry Shortcake, *112*
Iced Vanilla, *93*

K
Knishes, Meat and Potato, *54–55*

L
LETTUCE
Panini Wraps, *24*
Peach and Mango Salad, *66*
Ramen Deli Salad, *48*

M
Malafel, *56*
Mango and Peach Salad, *66*
MARSHMALLOW
Erector Set, *140*
Rice Krispies Sandwiches, *122*
Meira's Pop'em Cookies, *106*
MEAT. *See also* **BEEF**
Taco Night, *44*
Meat and Potato Knishes, *54-55*
Micro-Dough, *138*
Muffins, Grab and Go, *86*
MUSHROOMS
Pita Packets, *26*
MUSTARD
Honey Dip, *72*
Meat and Potato Knishes, *54-55*
Roasted Dijon Potatoes, *64*

O
OATS
Chewy PB Granola Bars, *88*
Grab and Go Muffins, *86*
Meira's Pop'em Cookies, *106*
Onions, *8*
Onion n' Garlic Popcorn, *80*

P
Pancake "Sandwiches," *32*
Panini Wraps, *24*
PASTA AND NOODLES
Creamy Orzo, *18*
Penne Rosa, *16*
Ramen Deli Salad, *48*
Toasted Bow-Tie Chips, *82*
Peach and Mango Salad, *66*
PEANUT BUTTER
Chewy PB Granola Bars, *88*
Pizzelle Cake, *98, 126-127*
PEANUTS
Banana Sundae Cake, *100*
Peach and Mango Salad, *66*
Peas, Sugar Snap, and Edamame, *70*
Penne Rosa, *16*
PEPPER(S)
Hot Banana, *90*
Panini Wraps, *24*
Red, Dip, Veggie Sticks with, *68*
Pita Chips, *20*
Pita Packets, *26*
Pizza, Deep Dish Personal, *22*
Pizza Soup, *20*
Pizzelle Cake, Peanut Butter, *98*
PLAY-DOUGH
Micro-Dough, *138*
Popcorn, Onion n' Garlic, *80*
POTATO(ES)
Chicken over French Fries, *42*
and Meat Knishes, *54–55*
Roasted Dijon, *64*
Two-, Oven Fries, *62*

Q
POULTRY. *See* **CHICKEN; TURKEY**
Pretzel Bars, Chocolate, *110*
Pretzels, Hot, *78*
Purple Salad, *57*

Quesadillas, Spinach, *28*

R
Ramen Deli Salad, *48*
Razzle, Ice Cream, *114*
Rice Krispies Sandwiches, *122*
Roasted Dijon Potatoes, *64*
Rugelach, Sour Gummy, *108*

S
SALADS
Peach and Mango, *66*
Purple, *57*
Ramen Deli, *48*
Salsa, Taco Chips and, *84*
Sand Art, Edible, *136*
SANDWICHES
Malafel, *56*
Panini Wraps, *24*
Pita Packets, *26*
Sino Steak, *46–47*
Spinach Quesadillas, *28*
"Sandwiches," Pancake, *32*
SAUCES. *See* **DIPS AND SAUCES**
Shortcake, Strawberry, *112*
Skinny Berry Coolata, *92*
Sorbets, Creamsicle, with Chocolate Wafer Pops, *120*
Soup, Pizza, *20*
Sour Gummy Rugelach, *108*
Spinach Quesadillas, *28*

STRAWBERRY(IES)
Pancake "Sandwiches," *32*
Shortcake, *112*
Skinny Berry Coolata, *92*
syrup, *32*

T
Taco Chips and Salsa, *84*
Taco Night, *44*
TAHINI PASTE
Techineh, *57*
Tartar Sauce, *59*
Teriyaki Beef Sticks, *50*
Toasted Bow-Tie Chips, *82*
Toffee-Topped Brownie Cake, *96*
TOMATOES
DIY Barbecue Sauce, *40*
Penne Rosa, *16*
Pizza Soup, *20*
Ramen Deli Salad, *48*
Taco Chips and Salsa, *84*
Taco Night, *44*
TURKEY
Ramen Deli Salad, *48*
Two-Potato Oven Fries, *62*

V
VEGETABLES. *See also* **SPECIFIC VEGETABLES**
Veggie Sticks with Red Pepper Dip, *68*

W
WALNUTS
Candy Bar Cookies, *102*

Z
Zour Peg Solitaire, *140*
Zucchini Spaghetti, *74*